KAPLAN

TOEFL iBT®

Premium Plus

2027

4 PRACTICE TESTS + PROVEN STRATEGIES + AUDIO

HIGHER SCORE GUARANTEED

Special thanks to the team who made this book possible: Catherine Baum, Harry Broome, Matthew Callan, Scarlet Edmonds, Jo L'Abbate, Teresa Rupp, Amit Schlesinger, Nimesh Shah, Lisa Gefen Sicilian, Andrew La Voy, Jacob Zampier.

Published by Kaplan North America, LLC dba Kaplan Publishing
1515 West Cypress Creek Road
Fort Lauderdale, FL 33309

10 9 8 7 6 5 4 3 2 1

ISBN: 979-8-3497-0385-0

TABLE OF CONTENTS

▶ GO ONLINE
www.kaptest.com/booksonline

TABLE OF CONTENTS

CHAPTER 1

Introduction to the TOEFL iBT

Welcome to Kaplan

Congratulations on your decision to study for the TOEFL iBT, and welcome to your Kaplan TOEFL iBT preparation program. Kaplan is one of the world's largest, most diverse education providers. As a leader in test preparation, we have over 80 years of experience helping people conquer standardized tests and take a big step closer to achieving their dreams.

With our expertise, we've helped millions of students reach their educational and career goals. Raising test scores is our specialty, so you're in good hands. It may take hard work for you to master the TOEFL iBT, but you won't regret doing it, and Kaplan is here to help you as you prepare for this important step. Let's get you ready to start learning, practicing, and raising your score. Your program includes this book and the accompanying online resources. These work together to provide you with complete TOEFL iBT preparation in a variety of formats. We are excited to walk with you on your TOEFL iBT prep journey.

Exam Overview

The Test of English as a Foreign Language (TOEFL) is a standardized test designed to measure a student's ability to understand and use English as it is used in an academic setting, such as a university. Standardized tests are widely used in the United States for college and graduate school admissions and professional licensing. The TOEFL is produced and administered by the Educational Testing Service (ETS), a private, not-for-profit company based in Princeton, New Jersey.

The TOEFL has been around in some form since the 1960s. The TOEFL Internet-based test (iBT) in particular was launched in 2005. It was revised in 2019, again in 2023, and most recently in January of 2026. You can choose to take the TOEFL iBT at a test center or at home with a live proctor.

The questions on the test take about 2 hours to complete, though it is an Adaptive Test, so the length is variable based on how you answer the questions. Expect the entire test to take around 2 1/2 hours, including directions. The TOEFL iBT consists of four sections: Reading, Listening, Writing, and Speaking.

SECTION	QUESTIONS	TIMING
Reading	Up to 50 questions	Up to 30 minutes
Listening	Up to 47 questions	Up to 29 minutes
Writing	12 questions	Up to 23 minutes
Speaking	11 questions	Up to 8 minutes

How the Exam Is Scored

Understanding your TOEFL iBT score is critical to achieving your academic goals. As of the **January 2026 update**, ETS has introduced a new scoring scale to provide a more intuitive alignment with the Common European Framework of Reference for Languages (CEFR).

The New 1–6 Band Scale

You will receive an **overall score on a scale of 1 to 6**, measured in half-point increments (e.g., 4.5, 5.0, 5.5). Your overall score is the average of your four section scores, also reported on the 1–6 scale.

Before January 21, 2026, overall scores were reported on a 0–120 scale. Between 2026 and 2028, in order to help institutions transition to the current 1–6 scoring system, score reports will display both the new 1–6 band score and the traditional 0–120 total score side by side.

Scoring Breakdown by Section

ETS uses a combination of automated artificial intelligence (AI) technology and highly trained human raters to ensure fair and accurate results.

- **Reading & Listening (Scored by Computer):** These sections are scored based on the number of correct responses. Because the test is adaptive, the computer accounts for the difficulty of the questions you were served to determine your final scaled score.
- **Speaking (AI + Human Raters):** Your responses are evaluated for fluency, pronunciation, delivery, language use, and topic development.
- **Writing (AI + Human Raters):** Your responses are evaluated for grammatical accuracy, vocabulary variety, and how well you support your ideas.

What Your Scores Mean

Your score report will categorize your proficiency into levels. Below is how the current 1–6 scale aligns with institutional expectations:

TOEFL BAND	CEFR LEVEL	PROFICIENCY DESCRIPTION
5.5 – 6.0	C1 – C2	**Advanced/Proficient:** Meets requirements for many highly competitive programs.
4.5 – 5.0	B2 – C1	**High-Intermediate:** Meets requirements for most graduate and undergraduate programs.
3.5 – 4.0	B1 – B2	**Intermediate:** Meets requirements for many colleges.

How This Book Is Organized

This book has four sections, corresponding to the four sections of the TOEFL iBT and appearing in the same order that the sections appear on the exam: Reading, Listening, Writing, and Speaking. Each section of the book describes strategies for all of the question types and tasks on the TOEFL iBT.

Practice and Strategy

The strategies are followed by practice exercises, so you can apply specific techniques to each question type. The answer key contains the answers for fill-in-the-blank and multiple-choice questions as well as sample responses for Writing and Speaking tasks. It is recommended that you work through all four sections of the book in order to learn and practice the skills and strategies that will help you to succeed on Test Day.

Academic Realism

The sample passages and practice activities cover similar academic fields as the TOEFL iBT: history, hard sciences (physics, chemistry, etc.), education, business and economics, social sciences, arts and literature, and technology. Like the topics on the actual test, the topics in this book are mixed, meaning they are not grouped by field. This ensures your learning experience is varied and represents the actual academic level of the test.

Your Online Companion

Many practice exercises in this book require listening to lectures or conversations. These are included in your **Online Companion**.

- The book will tell you when you must listen to a recording.
- Instructions will indicate track numbers, such as: *"Listen to **Audio File #1** in your online companion."*

When you are ready to put everything together, use the **four practice tests** in your Online Companion to practice for the testing experience.

CHAPTER 2

Reading

The Reading section occurs first on the TOEFL iBT. In this section, you will see up to 50 questions in total, made up of three *types* of questions: Complete the Words, Read in Daily Life, and Read an Academic Passage. We will go over each of these question types in depth in this chapter and share some helpful strategies along the way. At the end of the chapter are more practice questions followed by their answers and explanations.

Question Type: Complete the Words

Complete the Words questions target your ability to process written texts for meaning and form.

You will see an academic text about the length of a paragraph, or about 70–100 words. The first sentence will always be complete. Then, for the next 20 words starting at the beginning of the second sentence, every *other* word will be missing letters. Thus, 10 words in total will have missing letters. The missing letters will always be the letters that make up the second half of the words. Your job is to figure out the missing letters and type them into the correct spaces.

You can go in any order you want, though you will generally find it easier to begin with the first missing letter and continue from start to finish.

Here is an example:

Directions: Read the text below. Some words are missing their endings. Complete each word by filling in the missing letters in the spaces provided.

Passage:

The stunning rings of Saturn are not solid structures, but are instead composed of billions of separate particles orbiting the planet. The si_ _ of ea_ _ of th_ _ _ individual obj_ _ _ _ ranges fr_ _ tiny spe_ _ _ to la_ _ _ boulders, wh_ _ _ their compo_ _ _ _ _ _ is mos_ _ _ water. The sheer vastness and delicate structure of the rings make them one of the most beautiful sights in our solar system.

To do well on a *Complete the Words* question, begin by reading the entire passage once. At this stage, your goal is simply to understand the general topic and scope. In this example, you can quickly identify that the passage is about Saturn's rings and their structure. That's all you need for now.

Next, focus carefully on the first sentence. This sentence is always complete for a reason: it provides essential context that helps you infer the missing words in the following sentence or sentences. Here, the first sentence tells us that Saturn's rings are made up of many "separate particles." This suggests that the second sentence will continue describing these particles. It might discuss their composition, origin, size, or other characteristics. What's important is that you have context and can approach the next sentence more strategically.

When you move on to the second sentence, start by reading only the fully visible words. In this example, you can see words like *individual, ranges, tiny, boulders, their,* and *water.* From *ranges* and *tiny,* it becomes clear that the first part of the sentence is discussing how large the "separate particles" are, so it is reasonable to predict that the first word with missing letters is *size.*

As you identify likely words, fill them in, even if you are not completely sure about spelling yet. Focus first on meaning. At this point, the sentence begins to take shape:

The size of ea_ _ of th_ _ _ individual obj_ _ _ _ ranges fr_ _ tiny spe_ _ _ to la_ _ _ boulders

There is no fixed order for solving the rest of the sentence. You can work sequentially or skip around, depending on what feels easiest. Often, it is helpful to focus on phrases rather than individual words. For example, consider the phrase:

ranges fr_ _ tiny spe_ _ _ to la_ _ _ boulders

The structure *ranges from X to Y* is common, so *fr_ _* is likely *from.* Since the sentence contrasts *tiny* items with *boulders, la_ _ _* is likely *large.* Now the first part of the sentence becomes:

The size of ea_ _ of th_ _ _ individual obj_ _ _ _ ranges from tiny spe_ _ _ to large boulders

As you continue, each solved word makes the remaining ones easier. If you get stuck, shift your attention to another part of the sentence and return later. Every new word you confirm improves your understanding of the overall structure.

After completing all the words, take a moment to check spelling carefully. Finally, read the entire passage one more time to ensure it flows naturally and makes sense before moving on.

Answer Key and Explanation

The stunning rings of Saturn are not solid structures, but are instead composed of billions of separate particles orbiting the planet. The size of each of these individual objects ranges from tiny specks to large boulders, while their composition is mostly water. The sheer vastness and delicate structure of the rings make them one of the most beautiful sights in our solar system.

Here are the completed words for the passage:

SEQUENCE	PARTIAL WORD	FULL WORD	EXPLANATION
1	si_ _	**size**	The sentence contrasts *tiny* items with *boulders*, indicating a discussion of particle dimension, which is further supported by the preceding word *The* and the later word *ranges*.
2	ea_ _	**each**	The context requires a word referring to an individual particle, fitting the construction "of each of these individual objects."
3	th_ _ _	**these**	This is part of the phrase "of these individual objects," which refers back to the "separate particles" mentioned in the first sentence.
4	obj_ _ _ _	**objects**	This serves as a synonym for the "separate particles" being described in the sentence.
5	fr_ _	**from**	This completes the common phrase structure "*ranges from* X to Y," describing the scope of sizes.
6	spe_ _ _	**specks**	This word is a small, specific item that is contrasted with *boulders* and is preceded by the word *tiny*.

Continued

7	la___	**large**	This word is used to describe the second item in the size range, *boulders*, and is contrasted with *tiny specks*.
8	wh___	**while**	This word creates a transitional clause that introduces a new detail about the particles, connecting the size description to the composition.
9	compo______	**composition**	The context, especially the final word *water*, suggests a discussion of what the particles are chemically made of.
10	mos___	**mostly**	This word is a common adverb used to qualify the purity of the material, indicating that the composition is almost entirely *water*.

Question Type: Read in Daily Life

Read in Daily Life questions target your ability to understand the types of short, *nonacademic* texts that people commonly come across in daily life.

Each *Read in Daily Life* question will display such a text, consisting of no more than 150 words and sometimes as few as 15 words, and then present you with two or three multiple-choice questions.

There are many types of texts that might appear in *Read in Daily Life* questions, such as signs, advertisements, schedules, receipts, emails, articles, web pages, or social media posts. Regardless of the text, you need to be able to identify the main purpose of the text, understand the information within, understand any informal language it might contain, such as idiomatic expressions, and perhaps make inferences based on the text. This might sound like a complicated, formal list of skills, but keep in mind that the texts are all nonacademic and are the kinds of texts you regularly encounter in your life right now.

Here is an example with one practice question:

Office Kitchen Rules

Attention All Staff: To keep our breakroom clean and pleasant for everyone, please follow these simple rules:

- **Labels:** All food stored in the communal refrigerator must be clearly marked with your name and the date.
- **Friday Clean-out:** Every Friday at 4:00 PM, the refrigerator is emptied completely. Any items without a label or that have expired will be thrown away.
- **Microwaves:** Please cover your food while heating to prevent splattering. If a spill occurs, wipe it up immediately using the paper towels provided.
- **Dishes:** Do not leave dirty dishes in the sink. Wash them immediately or place them in the dishwasher.

Question:

According to the notice, what will happen to a container of food left in the refrigerator on Friday afternoon?

A. It will be moved to the freezer if it does not have a date.

B. It will be washed by the cleaning staff if it is in a dirty dish.

C. It will be thrown away if a label is not written on it.

D. It will be kept until Monday morning if it has not yet expired.

Because of the great variety of texts that you might see, it's best that you have a general approach that you can apply to whatever type of text you are given.

We recommend you read the text in two passes.

First, skim the text quickly and then ask yourself the following three questions:

1. Who probably wrote it?
2. Who is it written for?
3. What is its overall purpose?

In our sample text, this appears to have been written by an office manager or other staff in charge of the breakroom. The intended target, as stated in the notice, is all of the staff. The overall purpose is to set forth the kitchen rules for the breakroom.

Next, read through the text a little more carefully to familiarize yourself with the basic ideas expressed. Don't read for detail, and don't spend too much time on this step. Here, you can see that cleanliness is the overall concern. The stated rules involve labeling food in the refrigerator, emptying the refrigerator on Fridays, keeping the microwave oven clean, and not leaving dishes in the sink.

After your second pass, move on to the questions. Once you read a question stem, return to the text and focus on the relevant details. Try to formulate the correct answer in your head before looking at the answer choices.

Answer and Explanation:

Correct Choice:

- Our sample question asks about a container of food left in the refrigerator on Friday afternoon. The text states that during the Friday clean-out at 4:00 PM, any items "without a label" will be thrown away. This makes Choice C correct.

Incorrect Choices:

- Choice A: The notice does not mention a freezer or moving food to different locations; it only mentions emptying the refrigerator and throwing items away.
- Choice B: The "Dishes" rule tells employees to wash their own dishes or use the dishwasher; it does not say that staff will wash them for you, especially not those left in the refrigerator.
- Choice D: The text says the refrigerator is emptied "completely" and that items without labels or those that are expired are tossed. It does not suggest that unlabeled items are granted an extension until Monday.

Question Type: Read an Academic Passage

Read an Academic Passage questions present you with a short expository passage similar to those used in secondary and higher education. The passage will be about 200 words long and will discuss something from the humanities (e.g., art, music, literature), social sciences (e.g., economics, history), or the physical sciences (e.g., biology, physics).

After the passage, you will be asked five questions. The passage and questions are designed so that background knowledge of the topic is *not* required. Everything you need to answer the questions is right there in the passage, though you may be required to make inferences or think critically as you read.

The question may ask about details stated in the passage, inferences that can be drawn from the passage, the purpose of all or part of the passage, the meaning of vocabulary in context, or the relationship between ideas discussed in the passage.

Here is an example with one practice question:

The Phenomenon of Island Gigantism

In evolutionary biology, "island gigantism" refers to a biological phenomenon where the size of an animal species isolated on an island increases dramatically compared to its relatives on the mainland. This trend is most commonly observed in species that are naturally small, such as rodents, insects, or small reptiles. Several ecological factors contribute to this shift. Primarily, islands often lack the large mammalian predators found on continents. In the absence of such threats, small animals no longer need to remain tiny to hide in crevices or burrows; instead, they can grow larger to improve their own hunting capabilities or survival odds.

Furthermore, islands frequently have limited food resources but also less competition from other species. Larger body size can be a distinct advantage in these environments, as bigger animals can store more fat and survive longer periods of food scarcity. A classic example is the Dodo bird of Mauritius. Descended from small, flightless pigeons, the Dodo evolved into a much larger, heavier bird because it faced no natural predators in its island habitat. However, this specialization also makes island giants highly vulnerable. When humans or invasive species are introduced to these isolated ecosystems, the "giants" often face rapid extinction because they have lost their defensive instincts and cannot adapt quickly to new threats.

Question:

According to the passage, why is a larger body size beneficial for animals living on islands with limited food resources?

A. It allows them to better compete with large mammalian predators for prey.

B. It enables them to hide more effectively in burrows during periods of scarcity.

C. It provides the ability to store energy reserves to survive when food is hard to find.

D. It helps them develop the defensive instincts necessary to ward off invasive species.

One thing to keep in mind is that the passage remains on the screen when you answer the questions. There's no need to try to memorize all of the details from the passage, since you can simply look up information that you are asked about. You will be referring to the passage a number of times as you work through the five questions.

Therefore, your strategy when you initially read the passage is to focus on the big picture. Try to get a handle on the main ideas of the passage, the structure (how it's put together, what each paragraph is doing in the passage), and the author's overall purpose.

In our sample, the passage explains the concept of island gigantism, why it happens, and its consequences. The first paragraph introduces the concept and explains why island gigantism happens. The second paragraph discusses some advantages of island gigantism, gives the example of the dodo, and discusses a downside of island gigantism. Overall, the author's purpose is to explain and illustrate the concept of island gigantism. The author isn't trying to persuade or argue, but to inform and explain.

That's all you need to get out of this passage at first. Move on to the questions and be prepared to research details.

Answer and Explanation:

Our sample question asks why a larger body size is beneficial for animals living on islands with limited food resources. Recall that the second paragraph discusses advantages of island gigantism, so start researching there. The first sentence mentions that islands often have limited food resources. The second sentence explains that larger body size can be helpful in these environments, because bigger animals can store more fat and survive longer periods of food scarcity. Now scan the answer choices for a match.

Correct Choice:

- Choice C: The passage explicitly states that on islands with limited food, "bigger animals can store more fat and survive longer periods of food scarcity." Choice C directly paraphrases this information by mentioning the storage of energy reserves.

Incorrect Choices:

- Choice A: The passage states that islands often lack large mammalian predators; therefore, the animals are not competing with them.
- Choice B: The text says that animals no longer need to hide in burrows because of the absence of predators, and it connects larger size to survival during scarcity, not to hiding.
- Choice D: The passage actually says the opposite—that these animals lose their defensive instincts and are vulnerable to invasive species. Large size is not described as a way to develop these instincts.

General Strategies

In general, here are some strategies to help you while you answer questions in the reading section.

1. Let the Purpose Dictate Your Pace

One of the biggest mistakes students make is reading a 15-word daily life sign at the same speed as a 200-word academic passage. For *Read in Daily Life* questions, you should be a "scanner." Your goal is to find the specific rule or constraint (like the Friday refrigerator clean-out rule) and ignore the rest. For *Read an Academic Passage* questions, you should read to understand the relationship between parts of the passage, especially the relationship between paragraphs—for example, how the first paragraph introduces a theory and the second provides an example (like the Dodo bird) that supports or challenges it.

2. Practice "The Process of Elimination"

TOEFL is famous for "distractors"—wrong answers that look right because they use words found in the text. Instead of looking for the "right" answer, actively hunt for why three of the options are **wrong**. If a choice adds information not in the text, contradicts a detail, or is "too broad," cross it out.

3. Master the "Direct Restatement" Rule

For almost every detail question, the correct answer is a **paraphrase**. This means the test will take a sentence from the passage and rewrite it using different words with the same meaning. Developing a strong bank of synonyms is your best defense against the test's attempts to trick you.

4. Manage Your "Mental Budget"

You don't need to be an expert in biology, history, or economics to pass. Everything you need is on the screen. A helpful mental strategy is to treat the passage like a "closed loop." If an answer choice sounds like something you heard in a different class or read in a news article, but it isn't in the text provided, it is a trap. Stay strictly within the boundaries of the provided text, and you will avoid the common pitfall of "over-thinking" or using outside knowledge that the test didn't intend for you to use.

More Practice

Question 1: Complete the Words

Directions: Read the text below. Some words are missing their endings. Complete each word by filling in the missing letters into the spaces provided.

Passage:

The tropical rainforest is Earth's most diverse biome, housing millions of unique species within its dense, green canopy. Bec _ _ _ _ of th_ _ high rain_ _ _ _, these for _ _ _ _ stay lu_ _ year-ro_ _ _. Many ani _ _ _ _ live entir_ _ _ in t_ _ trees, ne_ _ _ touching the ground. This vertical layering allows many different creatures to coexist in the same small geographic area.

Question 2: Complete the Words

Directions: Read the text below. Some words are missing their endings. Complete each word by filling in the missing letters into the spaces provided.

Passage:

Cognitive psychology explores the internal mental processes required to perceive, remember, and speak. This discip_ _ _ _ investigates h_ _ people acqu_ _ _ information throu_ _ sensory inp_ _ and st_ _ _ it f_ _ later retr_ _ _ _ _. Modern experim_ _ _ _ use th_ _ data to map human intelligence.

Questions 3 and 4: Read in Daily Life

Returns and Exchanges Thank you for shopping at Quick-Stop! If you are not satisfied with your purchase, please review our policy:

- **Deadline:** Returns must be made within 14 days of the purchase date.
- **Condition:** Items must be in their original packaging and include all accessories (chargers, manuals, etc.).
- **Receipt:** A valid paper or digital receipt is required for all cash refunds.
- **Store Credit:** Items returned without a receipt, or returns made between 15 and 30 days after purchase, will receive store credit only.
- **Exclusions:** Opened software and headphones cannot be returned for hygiene and copyright reasons.

Question 3:

What is required to receive a cash refund?

A. Returning the item within 30 days.

B. Bringing the original receipt.

C. Exchanging the item for software.

D. Returning headphones in their original box.

Question 4:

What happens if a customer returns a laptop in its box 20 days after buying it?

A. They will receive a full cash refund.

B. They will be denied a return because it is too late.

C. They will receive store credit instead of cash.

D. They can exchange it for a pair of headphones.

Questions 5–9: Read an Academic Passage

The Printing Revolution in Europe

Before the mid-fifteenth century, European books were painstakingly hand-copied by scribes, a process that made them rare, expensive, and prone to human error. This changed dramatically with Johannes Gutenberg's invention of the movable-type printing press around 1440. By adapting technology from wine and olive presses and developing a unique metal alloy for type, Gutenberg allowed for the rapid, uniform reproduction of texts.

The implications of this shift were profound. As the cost of books plummeted, literacy rates—previously confined to the clergy and the wealthy elite—began to rise among the merchant and middle classes. The availability of information in vernacular languages, rather than just Latin, further accelerated this trend. Furthermore, the printing press played a critical role in the Scientific Revolution. Scientists could now share their findings with a wider audience, ensuring that their data remained consistent across thousands of copies. This "standardization" of knowledge meant that researchers in different countries could build upon each other's work with greater accuracy. However, the rapid spread of ideas also posed a challenge to established authorities. For the first time, dissenting political and religious views could be distributed faster than they could be suppressed, fundamentally altering the power dynamics of European society.

Question 5:

What was a primary limitation of books produced before the invention of the printing press?

A. They were frequently written in vernacular languages.

B. They were expensive and contained many mistakes.

C. They were primarily used by the merchant class.

D. They were produced using modified wine presses.

Question 6:

The word "profound" in the second paragraph is closest in meaning to:

A. Hidden

B. Significant

C. Difficult

D. Ancient

Question 7:

How did the printing press facilitate the Scientific Revolution?

A. By encouraging scientists to write only in Latin.

B. By making it harder for researchers to build on previous work.

C. By suppressing dissenting religious and political views.

D. By ensuring that data was consistent across many copies.

Question 8:

Which of the following can be inferred about literacy before the 1440s?

A. Literacy was largely limited to specific social groups.

B. Standardized knowledge was already common across Europe.

C. Most middle-class merchants were highly literate.

D. Scientific findings were shared rapidly using metal alloys.

Question 9:

Why does the author mention "established authorities" at the end of the passage?

A. To suggest they were the primary inventors of the press.

B. To explain why they encouraged the use of vernacular languages.

C. To highlight a social conflict caused by the rapid spread of information.

D. To show how they used the press to improve power dynamics.

Questions 10–14: Read an Academic Passage

Deep-Sea Hydrothermal Vents

For decades, biologists believed that all life on Earth ultimately depended on sunlight for energy through the process of photosynthesis. However, the discovery of hydrothermal vents in 1977 on the ocean floor near the Galápagos Rift fundamentally challenged this assumption. These vents are essentially underwater geysers located along mid-ocean ridges where tectonic plates are pulling apart. As seawater seeps into the Earth's crust, it is heated by magma and becomes enriched with dissolved minerals and gases, such as hydrogen sulfide, before being ejected back into the freezing depths.

In this pitch-black environment, where temperatures can reach 400°C, vibrant ecosystems thrive. Instead of sunlight, the foundation of this food web is a process called chemosynthesis. Specialized bacteria oxidize the chemical compounds in the vent fluid to produce energy, effectively replacing the role of plants. These bacteria support a diverse array of life, including giant tube worms, which can grow up to two meters long, and unique species of eyeless shrimp. Because these ecosystems are isolated from the rest of the biosphere, they offer scientists a rare glimpse into how life might have originated on early Earth or even how it might exist on other icy moons in our solar system, such as Jupiter's Europa.

Question 10:

What was the scientific significance of discovering hydrothermal vents?

A. It proved that tectonic plates move closer together over time.

B. It showed that life could exist without relying on energy from the sun.

C. It confirmed that seawater stays at a constant temperature in the crust.

D. It demonstrated that photosynthesis can occur in pitch-black environments.

Question 11:

The word "enriched" in the first paragraph is closest in meaning to:

A. Cleaned

B. Expensive

C. Cooled

D. Enhanced

Question 12:

According to the passage, how do chemosynthetic bacteria differ from plants?

A. They grow much larger than typical plant species.

B. They survive by consuming eyeless shrimp.

C. They use chemical compounds rather than sunlight to produce energy.

D. They can only exist in freezing water.

Question 13:

Why does the author mention giant tube worms and eyeless shrimp?

A. To provide examples of species that have migrated from the surface.

B. To argue that these animals are dangerous to humans.

C. To illustrate the diversity of life supported by chemosynthetic bacteria.

D. To explain how animals protect themselves from 400°C temperatures.

Question 14:

What can be inferred about the moon Europa based on the passage?

A. It is a volcanic planet with no water.

B. It may have conditions that could support life similar to hydrothermal vents.

C. Humans have already discovered eyeless shrimp there.

D. It is the only place in the solar system with tectonic plates.

Answers and Explanations

Question 1:

SEQUENCE	FRAGMENT	FULL WORD	LINGUISTIC EXPLANATION
1	Bec____	Because	A conjunction used to show cause. It explains why the forests are "lush."
2	th__	this	A demonstrative adjective modifying the amount of rainfall.
3	rain____	rainfall	A compound noun. In a rainforest context, "rain-" is almost always followed by "-fall."
4	for____	forests	The subject noun. Since we are talking about rainforests, this is the logical plural noun.
5	lu__	lush	An adjective meaning growing luxuriantly. It describes the state of the vegetation.
6	year-ro___	year-round	A compound adjective/adverb. It indicates the forests stay green through all seasons.
7	ani____	animals	The subject noun of the third sentence; the "unique species" mentioned earlier.
8	entir___	entirely	An adverb modifying "live." Many creatures live 100% of their lives in trees.
9	t__	the	A definite article. It specifies the trees mentioned in the canopy.
10	ne___	never	An adverb of frequency. High-canopy animals often never descend to the forest floor.

Question 2:

SEQUENCE	FRAGMENT	FULL WORD	LINGUISTIC EXPLANATION
1	discip____	discipline	A noun used here as a synonym for "field" within science.
2	h__	how	An interrogative adverb used to introduce a subordinate clause of manner.
3	acqu___	acquire	A formal academic verb meaning to "get" or "obtain" (common in learning contexts).
4	throu__	through	A preposition indicating the means or medium by which something happens.
5	inp__	input	A noun referring to the data or signals received by a system/brain.
6	st___	store	A verb that completes the parallel structure: *acquire* and *store*.
7	f__	for	A preposition indicating the purpose or intended use of the stored info.
8	retr_____	retrieval	A noun (suffix *-val*) describing the act of recovering stored information.
9	experim____	experiments	A plural noun referring to the scientific tests conducted by researchers.
10	th__	this	A demonstrative adjective used to point back to the specific data mentioned.

Question 3:

Correct Choice:

- Choice B: The text specifically states, "A valid paper or digital receipt is required for all cash refunds."

Incorrect Choices:

- Choice A is wrong because a cash refund is only available within 14 days (after that, it's store credit).
- Choice C is wrong because software is listed as an "exclusion."
- Choice D is wrong because headphones are explicitly listed as items that "cannot be returned."

Question 4:

Correct Choice:

- Choice C: The policy says that returns made "between 15 and 30 days after purchase will receive store credit only." Since 20 days falls into this window, store credit is the result.

Incorrect Choices:

- Choice A is wrong because 20 days is past the 14-day cash deadline.
- Choice B is wrong because the store *does* allow returns up to 30 days (for store credit).
- Choice D is wrong because the text doesn't suggest specific exchange rules for headphones, which are generally nonreturnable.

Question 5:

Correct Choice:

- Choice B: The first sentence of the passage states that before the press, books were "rare, expensive, and prone to human error." Choice B perfectly summarizes these two points.

Incorrect Choices:

- Choices A and C are incorrect because vernacular use and merchant literacy happened *after* the press was invented.
- Choice D is incorrect because it really isn't relevant to the question.

Question 6:

Correct Choice:

- Choice B: In this context, "profound" describes the "implications" of the printing press. Since the author goes on to describe major changes to literacy, science, and power structures, "significant" is the best synonym for an impact of this scale.

Incorrect Choices:

- Choice A is incorrect because the implications of the shift caused by the printing press were quite obvious, not "hidden."
- Choice C is incorrect because the author did not describe the implications of the shift caused by the printing press as "difficult" in any way, except perhaps that they were difficult for established authorities to accept. But the paragraph focuses on how significant the changes were overall, not just how the established authorities reacted.
- Choice D, "ancient," does not make sense in the context of the second paragraph.

Question 7:

Correct Choice:

- Choice D: The text explains that the press allowed scientists to ensure their data "remained consistent across thousands of copies," leading to the "standardization of knowledge." This allowed researchers to build on work with more accuracy.

Incorrect Choices:

- Choice A is incorrect because the passage does not at all indicate that scientists wrote in Latin. The only time Latin is mentioned is when Paragraph 2 states that the printing press led to the availability of information in "vernacular languages, rather than just Latin." If anything, this would suggest that scientists might have NOT written only in Latin.
- Choice B is a 180, meaning the opposite of what the passage states. According to paragraph 2, the printing press led to standardization of knowledge that meant that researchers COULD build on previous work.
- Choice C is outside the scope, as dissenting religious and political views were not mentioned in relation to the Scientific Revolution, but simply as a separate implication of the printing press.

Question 8:

Correct Choice:

- Choice A: The passage states that before the press, literacy was "confined to the clergy and the wealthy elite." This allows us to infer that it was limited to specific groups rather than being widespread.

Incorrect Choices:

- Choice B is contradicted by the passage, which indicates that the printing press led to standardization of knowledge. That implies that before the printing press, standardization did NOT exist.
- Choice C is contradicted by the passage, which indicates that the printing press led to literacy rates rising among the merchant class. That implies that before the printing press literacy rates were NOT high.
- Choice D is a distortion of the passage text. Paragraph 1 states that Gutenberg used a unique metal alloy for the printing press type, not that scientific findings were shared using metal alloys.

Question 9:

Correct Choice:

- Choice C: The final paragraph discusses how the spread of "dissenting political and religious views" posed a "challenge" to these authorities. The author includes this to show that the printing press didn't just spread data; it created conflict by changing how power was held in society.

Incorrect Choices:

- Choice A is a distortion, as paragraph 1 indicates that Gutenberg was the inventor of the press.
- Choice B is also a distortion. The established authorities did not encourage the use of any particular language. The author merely states in paragraph 2 that the press led to the availability of information in vernacular languages.
- Choice D is incorrect because the established authorities did not use the press to do anything. It was the use of the press for the general population that led to the spread of views that ended up altering the power dynamics.

Question 10:

Correct Choice:

- Choice B: The passage explains that before 1977, it was believed all life needed sunlight. The discovery of these vents "fundamentally challenged" that, showing life could thrive via chemosynthesis in the dark.

Incorrect Choices:

- Choice A is incorrect because although the passage mentions tectonic plates, it doesn't even deal with their long-term movement toward each other.
- Choice C must be rejected because the passage actually says seawater is heated, not constant in temperature.
- Choice D is incorrect because photosynthesis requires sunlight; the passage introduces chemosynthesis instead.

Question 11:

Correct Choice:

- Choice D: As seawater seeps into the crust, it picks up minerals and gases. Its chemical makeup is "enhanced" or "augmented" by these additions. In a scientific context, to enrich something is to increase the concentration of certain elements within it.

Incorrect Choices:

- Choice A would mean things are removed, the opposite of what's happening.
- Choice B is not related to the scientific context.
- Choice C is incorrect because the water is actually heated.

Question 12:

Correct Choice:

- Choice C: The text defines the difference clearly: plants use sunlight (photosynthesis), while these bacteria "oxidize the chemical compounds in the vent fluid to produce energy" (chemosynthesis).

Incorrect Choices:

- Choice A is incorrect because the passage does not compare their size.
- Choice B is incorrect because the bacteria support other organisms; they don't consume shrimp.
- Choice D is incorrect because the passage mentions extreme environments, but not that they only exist in freezing water.

Question 13:

Correct Choice:

- Choice C: These animals are listed as part of the "vibrant ecosystems" that rely on the bacteria. They serve as evidence that a full, complex food web can exist without any input from the sun.

Incorrect Choices:

- Choice A is incorrect because the passage does not say these species migrated from the surface.
- Choice B is incorrect because there is no mention of danger to humans.
- Choice D is incorrect because the passage does not explain how these animals handle extreme temperatures.

Question 14:

Correct Choice:

- Choice B: The final sentence states that vents offer a glimpse into how life "might exist" on Europa. This allows us to infer that scientists suspect Europa has similar conditions—such as liquid water and chemical energy sources—that could support life.

Incorrect Choices:

- Choice A is incorrect because the passage does not describe Europa as volcanic or lacking water.
- Choice C is incorrect because there is no claim that life has already been discovered there.
- Choice D is incorrect because the passage does not compare Europa to other places in terms of tectonic plates.

CHAPTER 3

Listening

The Listening section is the second section you will see on the TOEFL iBT. In this section, you will see up to 47 questions in total, appearing in four different *types* of tasks. These tasks are Listen and Choose a Response, Listen to a Conversation, Listen to an Announcement, and Listen to an Academic Talk. We will go over each of these question types in depth in this chapter and share some helpful strategies along the way. At the end of the chapter are more practice questions followed by their answers and explanations.

Question Type: Listen and Choose a Response

The *Listen and Choose a Response* task is designed to measure your ability to understand a short, spoken question or statement and recognize an appropriate response. The topic of the question or statement will be something related to campus life.

You will first hear a question or statement. You will only hear it; it will not be written on the screen. Then, on the screen, you will see four possible responses to the question or statement. You have to choose the most appropriate response to the speaker's question or statement.

Here's an example of the type of question you might hear, along with the answer choices: Again, on the TOEFL iBT you will only *hear* the question, not see it. You *will* see the answer choices, however.

Example:

Listen to ***Audio File #1*** *in your online companion.*

The Audio (What you will hear online):

> *"I heard the professor is moving the deadline for the research paper up to this Friday—did you catch that too?"*

To select the appropriate choice for a *Listen and Choose a Response* task, you must be able to understand both the literal meaning of what the speaker says and any implied meanings. In other words, you not only have to understand vocabulary, phrases, and common grammatical structures such as question-formation patterns, but you also have to recognize the meaning of common voice intonation and stress patterns and any meanings that the speaker is implying. These are all skills that are important for social interactions.

In this example question, pay close attention to the **verb phrase** "moving the deadline up." In a campus context, this means the task is now due *sooner* than originally planned. Understanding these common phrasal verbs is essential for identifying the speaker's tone—usually one of surprise or concern.

The question was asked in the audio. Here are the possible responses (answers):

A. I've already submitted my application for the research grant.

B. The professor usually posts the syllabus on the student portal.

C. Wait, really? I thought we had until next Wednesday to finish it.

D. Friday is typically the busiest day at the campus library.

Answer Key and Explanation

Correct Choice:

- Choice C: To answer correctly, you must recognize the speaker's intent. The speaker is sharing a piece of potentially stressful news (the "moving up" of a deadline) and asking for confirmation ("did you catch that too?"). Choice (C) is the only logical response because it acknowledges the news and provides a reaction that fits the context of a student who was under a different impression regarding the due date.

Incorrect Choices:

- Choice A confuses "research paper" with "research grant." While the topics are academic, a grant application is unrelated to a classroom assignment deadline. Choice B provides general information about where to find a syllabus, but it doesn't address the specific question about the sudden change in the deadline. Choice D mentions "Friday," which was in the prompt, but it shifts the topic to library foot traffic rather than addressing the urgency of the paper being due.

Question Type: Listen to a Conversation

The *Listen to a Conversation* task is designed to measure your ability to comprehend a conversation in modern academic situations.

You will first listen to a short conversation between two speakers. The conversation will be about everyday topics such as shopping, dining, health, hobbies, travel, social activities, education, entertainment, services, or communications. To understand the conversation well enough, you will need to be able to do more than just recognize the spoken words. You'll also have to make inferences and predictions, and recognize speaker roles and purposes.

After you listen to the conversation, you will have to answer two questions about it.

Here is an example with one practice question:

*Listen to **Audio File #4** in your online companion.*

The Audio (What you will hear online):

Narrator: *Listen to a conversation between two students in the student union.*
Male Student: *Hey Sarah! I didn't see you at the volunteer fair yesterday. I thought you were dying to sign up for the beach clean-up project?*
Female Student: *I was! But by the time I finished my chemistry lab, the fair was packing up. I guess my lab partner and I got a little too carried away with our titration experiment.*
Male Student: *That's too bad. The list filled up pretty fast, but I think they're still looking for people to coordinate the carpool for Saturday morning.*
Female Student: *Carpool coordinator? Honestly, I have enough trouble keeping my own schedule straight. I was really hoping to just get my hands dirty on the dunes.*

Male Student: *Well, why don't you email Professor Miller? He's overseeing the whole thing. Sometimes people drop out at the last minute because of midterms.*
Female Student: *That's a thought. I'll send him a note tonight—it's worth a shot, right?*

Question and Explanation:

What does the woman imply when she says: "Honestly, I have enough trouble keeping my own schedule straight"?

A. She is too busy with her chemistry lab to volunteer on Saturdays.

B. She does not think she would be good at organizing the transportation.

C. She prefers to drive herself to the beach rather than join a carpool.

D. She has forgotten what time the beach clean-up starts.

Correct Choice:

- Choice B: To answer this correctly, you must look past the literal words and understand the speaker's purpose. The male student suggests a specific role: "carpool coordinator." The female student responds by mentioning her struggle with her own schedule. This is a polite way of saying she lacks the organizational skills for a leadership/logistical role. Therefore, she implies she wouldn't be the right fit for that specific task.

Incorrect Choices:

- Choice A is a "distractor" that uses the word "chemistry lab" from earlier in the conversation. However, she already expressed that she *wants* to go to the beach; her lab only made her late to the fair. Choice C takes the word "carpool" literally but misses her point about her organizational abilities. She wants to be a worker on the beach ("get my hands dirty"), not a driver or an organizer. Choice D misinterprets her "schedule" comment. She isn't saying she forgot the time; she's saying she isn't good at managing time/schedules in general.

In TOEFL conversations, listen for idioms and metaphors. When the student said she wanted to "get her hands dirty," she didn't literally mean she wanted dirt on her skin—she meant she wanted to do the physical work of the project rather than the administrative work. Identifying shifts in tone will help you catch the "implied" meanings.

Question Type: Listen to an Announcement

The *Listen to an Announcement* task is designed to simulate a common academic scenario in which you will find yourself: you are at a school-related event or in a classroom and an in-person or broadcasted message is being made. The message will pertain to rules and regulations, directions, schedules, student achievements, or other similar matters.

You will first listen to the short academic-related announcement. The announcement will be about 40 to 85 words long. Then you will answer questions about the announcement.

With *Listen to an Announcement* questions, picking the correct choice requires you to be able to identify the main ideas and basic context of the message, recognize the purpose of the speaker's message, and understand important details. Additionally, you must understand the range of grammatical structures used by proficient speakers, along with a wide range of vocabulary (including idioms and colloquial expressions). You might also be expected to infer meaning from what is stated and even predict future actions based on what the speaker has said in the announcement.

Here is an example with one practice question:

*Listen to **Audio File #7** in your online companion.*

The Audio (What you will hear online):

> ***Narrator:*** *Listen to an announcement from a university official.*
> ***Official:*** *"Attention all students currently residing in North Campus dormitories. Due to an unexpected water main break on Main Street, the city will be conducting emergency repairs starting tonight at 11:00 PM. As a result, water service to the Hillside and Riverside residence halls will be temporarily suspended for approximately six hours. We have set up a temporary station in the Student Union lobby, where bottled water and hand sanitizer are available free of charge until the repairs are completed. We apologize for the inconvenience and appreciate your patience as the city works to resolve this issue."*

Question and Explanation:

What is the main purpose of the announcement?

A. To inform students about a new water conservation policy on campus.

B. To explain why a campus social event in the Student Union was canceled.

C. To notify residents of a temporary utility disruption and provide resources.

D. To warn students to avoid the construction area on Main Street tonight.

Correct Choice:

- Choice C: This is a "big picture" question. The announcement covers a specific problem (water main break), the affected parties (Hillside and Riverside residents), and the solution/resource provided (bottled water at the Student Union). Choice C captures all these elements: the "utility disruption" (water suspension) and the "resources" (bottled water/sanitizer).

Incorrect Choices:

- Choice A is incorrect because the water shutoff is an emergency repair, not a permanent or long-term "policy" or conservation effort. Choice B is a "distractor" that mentions the Student Union, but the Union is being used as a distribution center, not a place where an event was canceled. Choice D focuses on the "construction area," but the primary purpose of the message is to help the students who won't have water in their dorms, not just to tell them where to walk.

In an announcement, the first sentence often identifies the "Who" (North Campus residents) and the middle explains the "What" and "Why" (water main break/repairs). The end often gives a "Call to Action" or a "Next Step" (go to the Student Union). If you miss the beginning, listen closely to the end—it often clarifies the entire purpose of the message.

Question Type: Listen to an Academic Talk

The *Listen to an Academic Talk* task is designed to simulate a common academic scenario in which you will find yourself: you are listening to an academic talk being given by an educator. The talk can be about any topic from the fields of history, art, music, life science, physical science, business and economics, or social science.

You are not expected to have any background knowledge in any of these subjects, however. Everything you need to answer the questions will come from what you hear.

With a *Listen to an Academic Talk* task, you will first listen to the short academic-related talk. The talk will be about 100 to 250 words long. Then you will answer four questions about the talk.

Here is an example with one practice question:

Listen to ***Audio File #10*** *in your online companion.*

The Audio (What you will hear online):

> ***Narrator:*** *Listen to a talk in a business and economics class.*
> ***Professor:*** *"When we look at why some companies thrive while others fail, we often turn to the 'Resource-Based View' of the firm. This theory suggests that a company's success isn't just about the industry it's in, but rather the unique resources it controls.*
> *To be a source of sustained competitive advantage, a resource must meet four specific criteria, often called the VRIO framework. First, the resource must be* ***Valuable****—it has to help the firm exploit an opportunity or neutralize a threat. Second, it must be* ***Rare****; if everyone has it, it's just a requirement for entry, not a competitive edge. Third, it must be* ***Inimitable****, meaning it's difficult or expensive for competitors to copy. And finally, the firm must be* ***Organized*** *to capture the value of that resource.*
> *Think of a company with a secret, world-class software algorithm. If that algorithm is valuable and rare, the company has a head start. But if a competitor can easily write a similar code by next week, that advantage is only temporary. It's the 'Inimitable' quality—the difficulty of duplication—that often separates a one-hit wonder from a market leader."*

Question and Explanation:

According to the professor, what determines if a company's advantage is "sustained" rather than just "temporary"?

A. Whether the company is operating in a high-tech industry.

B. The ability of the company to neutralize all market threats.

C. How difficult it is for other companies to replicate a resource.

D. The amount of money a company spends on new software algorithms.

Correct Choice:

- Choice C: The professor specifically highlights the "Inimitable" quality as the factor that separates a "temporary" advantage from a "sustained" one (a "market leader"). Choice C correctly identifies this by using the synonym "replicate" for "copy" or "duplicate."

Incorrect Choices:

- Choice A is incorrect because the professor states that success "isn't just about the industry it's in." Choice B mentions neutralizing threats, which relates to the "Valuable" criteria, but the professor does not link this specifically to the *duration* (sustained vs. temporary) of the advantage. Choice D focuses on the cost of the software, but the lecture emphasizes the *difficulty of duplication*, not the initial purchase price.

In academic talks, professors love to use **acronyms or frameworks** (like VRIO). When you hear a list of terms, try to jot down the first letter of each. More importantly, listen for the distinction the professor makes between those terms. In this talk, the "pivot point" was the difference between a "head start" (Valuable/Rare) and "sustained" success (Inimitable).

General Strategies

One of your major challenges as a TOEFL student is that you must do many things while listening. You cannot simply listen to a speaker or conversation in the relaxed, passive manner that you might listen to something in real life. You must listen actively, which means you have to constantly think about what you are hearing and analyze it as you are hearing it. If you do this well, you will not only find listening easier, but you'll find that you are in an excellent position to answer the questions with confidence. The first thing you want to do is be aware of your goals before you even start listening. Your ultimate goal is to be able to answer the questions correctly, so your listening goals relate to understanding those aspects of the lecture or conversation that you are likely to be asked about. Though you cannot know exactly what you will be asked, the TOEFL iBT asks the same kinds of questions on every test.

The more you focus on the following Strategies when listening, the better your chances are of answering all of the questions correctly:

1: Listen for and identify the purpose and main idea of the lecture or conversation.

Every professor has a goal for the lecture they give. Every student engaged in a conversation has something they are trying to achieve with that conversation. In most cases, we call the goal the speaker's Purpose. For example, a student's purpose in speaking with a professor might be to get an extension on their term paper. A professor's purpose in giving a lecture might be to argue that the Big Bang theory is likely to be correct.

2: Identify the key points or problems discussed.

Focus on key points, not minor details. As you continue to listen, your goal is to understand the key ideas being stated. How do you know what is a key idea? Once you know what the conversation or lecture is mainly about, or the purpose for the conversation or lecture (Strategy 1, above), you can anticipate certain types of points being discussed. Anticipating means thinking about what might or will come next, and it is a powerful part of active listening. For example, if you know a student has come to ask for an extension because something has gone wrong with his experiment, you can expect the student to describe what exactly has gone wrong. You can expect the professor to respond to those problems in detail. You can expect the professor to make a decision and to back it up with reasons. Anticipating the possibilities beforehand makes it easier to identify the actual key points when they are discussed. As you are listening, keep asking yourself, "What might they talk about next?" You'll find this makes listening easier and helps you focus on the key supporting points. And, when the speakers do bring up a new point, ask how it is connected to the main idea.

3: Try to infer meaning whenever possible.

To infer means to understand unstated ideas. Inference is involved in many question types on the TOEFL iBT. This is because meaning, organization, attitude, connections among ideas, and purpose are not always stated explicitly, but are implied. A speaker implies something when they communicate meaning indirectly. So, speakers often imply meaning, and it is your job as a listener to infer that meaning from what was actually said.

Consider the following conversation:

Man: Have you tried the steak in the cafeteria?
Woman: Actually, I'm a vegetarian.

The woman doesn't say directly that she didn't eat the steak, but she implies it by saying she's a vegetarian, a person who does not eat meat. Based on that fact, you can infer that she probably didn't try the steak.

A correct inference is always based on a stated idea. Listen for words that indicate the speaker's opinions or attitude toward what is being discussed. Of course, if a speaker says, "what I think . . ." or "it seems to me . . . ," then you know that the speaker's opinion is about to be expressed. But also pay attention to the speaker's tone of voice and use of strong language such as the words "especially," "crucial," "unfortunately," or "disappointing." These are strong clues about how a speaker feels or what their opinion is.

For example, imagine a speaker says,

> "The students voted last week on whether the conference should be held in the student union building or the main auditorium. Regrettably, the majority chose to have the conference in the student union building."

By the speaker's use of the word "regrettably," you can infer that the speaker wanted the conference to be held in the auditorium.

A good active listener constantly thinks of why the speaker said what they did and what they really meant by what they said.

More Practice

Question 1: Listen and Choose a Response

Directions: *Listen to **Audio File #2** in your online companion.*

Question:

The question was asked in the audio file. Here are the possible responses (answers):

A. The soccer stadium is located right next to the student union.

B. Most teams only practice once a week, so it's actually quite manageable.

C. I didn't know you were interested in becoming a professional athlete.

D. You should definitely check the library's hours before the final exam week.

Question 2: Listen and Choose a Response

Directions: *Listen to **Audio File #3** in your online companion.*

Question:

The question was asked in the audio file. Here are the possible responses (answers):

A. I think you should wait until next semester to take such a difficult class.

B. You actually need to go to the Math Department for that, not the registrar.

C. The registrar's office is open from nine to five every weekday.

D. I'm not sure if I have enough credits to graduate this spring either.

Questions 3 and 4: Listen to a Conversation

Directions: *Listen to **Audio File #5** in your online companion.* Once you have listened, answer the following questions.

Question 3:

Why was the textbook moved to the "Special Reserve" shelf?

A. The bookstore is running out of shelf space for political science books.

B. The professor requested that students only use the books inside the library.

C. It is a new edition that was recently added to the curriculum.

D. There was a mistake in the labeling of the "Global Politics" section.

Question 4:

What can be inferred about the student's decision?

A. She will likely choose the digital rental to save money.

B. She will buy the used online version despite the employee's warning.

C. She prefers physical books because she finds digital screens distracting.

D. She plans to wait until a used physical copy of the new edition becomes available.

Questions 5 and 6: Listen to a Conversation

Directions: *Listen to **Audio File #6** in your online companion.* Once you have listened, answer the following questions.

Question 5:

Why does the student visit the housing office?

A. To report that his roommate has already moved out of the dorm.

B. To complain about the housing office's assignment process.

C. To ask for a refund on his brother's housing deposit.

D. To request that a specific person be assigned to his room.

Question 6:

What does the coordinator imply when she says: "It's not as simple as just handing him the key"?

A. The student's brother is not allowed to have a key to the building.

B. There is a formal administrative process that must be followed.

C. The housing office has lost the keys to that specific dormitory.

D. The student is not authorized to help his brother with housing.

Questions 7 and 8: Listen to an Announcement

Directions: *Listen to **Audio File #8** in your online companion.* Once you have listened, answer the following questions.

Question 7:

What is the primary purpose of the announcement?

A. To invite students to a faculty luncheon on the third floor.

B. To explain the proper way to store laboratory equipment.

C. To announce new safety rules and a designated eating area.

D. To warn students that the chemistry wing is closed for finals.

Question 8:

What is the condition for using the third-floor study area?

A. Lab safety gear must be put away before entering.

B. Students must be accompanied by a faculty member.

C. Only bottled water is allowed in that specific room.

D. It is only available to students during normal business hours.

Questions 9 and 10: Listen to an Announcement

Directions: *Listen to* ***Audio File #9*** *in your online companion.* Once you have listened, answer the following questions.

Question 9:

What change is being made to the University Shuttle service?

A. The Gold Line is being replaced by a new express route.

B. The Blue Line will run more frequently during the morning.

C. A specific line is being temporarily stopped for repairs.

D. All shuttle services will be suspended until Friday afternoon.

Question 10:

What does the speaker suggest students do during the service change?

A. Walk to the Engineering Building instead of taking the bus.

B. Download a mobile application for live tracking.

C. Use the Student Health Center for parking.

D. Avoid traveling on the Gold Line during the afternoon.

Questions 11–14: Listen to an Academic Talk

Directions: *Listen to* ***Audio File #11*** *in your online companion.* Once you have listened, answer the following questions.

Question 11:

What is the main idea of the talk?

A. How to make silk using traditional Chinese methods.

B. The importance of the Silk Road for trade and culture.

C. The different types of tea sold in ancient Rome.

D. Why modern roads are better than ancient ones.

Question 12:

According to the professor, what made silk special?

A. It was the only thing people could use for money.

B. It was only produced in China for a long time.

C. It was used to make paper and gunpowder.

D. It was very easy and cheap to produce.

Question 13:

Why does the professor call the Silk Road a "cultural bridge"?

A. Because it was a literal bridge made of silk.

B. Because it helped spread religions and inventions.

C. Because it was used by builders to design new cities.

D. Because it allowed people to travel for vacations.

Question 14:

What was one item besides silk that was traded on these paths?

A. Roman statues
B. Cotton clothing
C. Spices
D. Gold coins

Questions 15–18: Listen to an Academic Talk

Directions: *Listen to* ***Audio File #12*** *in your online companion.* Once you have listened, answer the following questions.

Question 15:

What is the main focus of the professor's talk?

A. Why plants grow faster in cities than in the country.
B. The reasons why cities stay warmer than rural areas.
C. How to build stronger roads using asphalt and brick.
D. The history of air conditioning in large buildings.

Question 16:

According to the professor, why are dark surfaces like asphalt a problem?

A. They reflect too much sunlight into the eyes of drivers.
B. They are more expensive to repair than green spaces.
C. They soak up heat during the day and release it at night.
D. They prevent rainwater from reaching the roots of trees.

Question 17:

What is one benefit of "green roofs" mentioned in the lecture?

A. They provide extra space for people to grow their own food.
B. They make buildings look more modern and attractive.
C. They help reduce the temperature of the building.
D. They are easier to build than traditional roofs.

Question 18:

What does the professor imply about air conditioning use in cities?

A. It is the primary cause of the Urban Heat Island effect.
B. It is more expensive to run in the countryside.
C. It becomes more necessary because of trapped heat.
D. It will soon be replaced entirely by green roofs.

Answers and Explanations

Question 1:

Correct Choice:

- Choice B: In this scenario, the speaker is expressing a conflict between a desire (joining a sports league) and a responsibility (study time) and is seeking your opinion or advice ("What do you think?"). Choice B is the most appropriate response because it directly addresses the speaker's specific concern about "time." By providing information that the commitment is "manageable," it helps the speaker make a decision.

Incorrect Choices:

- Choice A provides geographical information about the stadium. While related to soccer, it does not address the speaker's dilemma regarding their schedule.
- Choice C misinterprets the scale of the activity. "Intramural" sports are recreational campus leagues for fun, not professional career paths, making this response illogical.
- Choice D focuses on the library and exams. While this relates to "study time," it doesn't give the speaker any feedback on whether they should join the soccer league.

In the *Listen and Choose a Response* task, look for **functional language**. In this prompt, the speaker is **seeking advice**. The correct answer will almost always provide that advice or provide information that helps the speaker solve their problem. Also, be careful with "distractor" answers like Choice A or D that use keywords from the prompt (soccer, study) but don't actually answer the question asked.

Question 2:

Correct Choice:

- Choice B: The speaker is expressing a specific problem (needing an "override") and asking for a location (the registrar) based on a common student assumption. Choice B is the best response because it corrects a factual misunderstanding in the campus workflow. In many universities, "departmental overrides" must be granted by the specific department teaching the course (in this case, Math or Statistics) before the registrar can finalize the enrollment.

Incorrect Choices:

- Choice A offers unsolicited advice about the difficulty of the course, which doesn't help the speaker solve the immediate technical problem of how to register.
- Choice C provides the office hours for the registrar. While this is related to the registrar, it doesn't address the fact that the registrar isn't actually the place the student needs to go for an *override*.
- Choice D shifts the conversation to the responder's own graduation concerns, failing to answer the speaker's question about where to go.

Listen for **specific terminology**. Words like "override," "prerequisite," "registrar," and "bursar" appear frequently in these tasks. If a speaker asks for a location to solve a specific problem, the correct answer often clarifies exactly which campus office handles that specific issue.

Question 3:

Correct Choice:

- Choice C: The employee explains that the book was moved because it is the newer edition the professor switched to.

Incorrect Choices:

- Choices A and D are incorrect interpretations of the physical location.
- Choice B is incorrect because "Special Reserve" in this bookstore context refers to the counter area, not a library-only policy.

Question 4:

Correct Choice:

- Choice A: The student states that "saving money is my top priority." While she mentions a preference for highlighting (which might suggest a physical book), her priority clearly points toward the most affordable option mentioned: the digital rental.

Incorrect Choices:

- Choice B is incorrect because she acknowledges the new regulations are important for exams.
- Choice C is incorrect because the student never says anything about digital screens being distracting.
- Choice D is incorrect because she needs the book now for the course.

When a conversation involves a conflict (e.g., wanting to save money vs. needing the correct edition), pay close attention to the final decision-making criteria. The TOEFL might test if you can identify which factor "wins" in the student's mind—in this case, her budget outweighed her preference for highlighting physical pages.

Question 5:

Correct Choice:

- Choice D: The student's primary motivation for the visit is to see if his brother (a "specific person") can take the empty spot in his room.

Incorrect Choices:

- Choice A is incorrect because the roommate is graduating in December (future), not already gone.
- Choices B and C are not mentioned in the dialogue.

Question 6:

Correct Choice:

- Choice B: The coordinator uses this phrase to signal that while the request is possible, there are official steps (applications, deposits, and mutual request forms) that must be completed first. It is an idiomatic way of saying "there is paperwork involved."

Incorrect Choices:

- Choices A, C, and D take the "key" or the "help" too literally and miss the metaphorical meaning of the coordinator's statement.

In TOEFL conversations, listen for conjunctions of contrast like "But" or "However." When the student says, *"But I was actually wondering . . ."* he is pivoting from the general situation (the roommate leaving) to his specific request (his brother moving in). This pivot almost always points directly to the answer for the "Purpose" question.

Question 7:

Correct Choice:

- Choice C: The speaker explicitly states the purpose is a "reminder regarding new safety protocols" (the rules) and mentions the conversion of the lounge (the designated area).

Incorrect Choices:

- Choice A is incorrect because "faculty lounge" refers to the location, not a lunch event.
- Choice B is a detail, not the primary purpose.
- Choice D is false: the labs aren't closed; they just have new rules.

Question 8:

Correct Choice:

- Choice A: The speaker says, "Please ensure all lab coats and safety goggles are stored in your assigned lockers before entering the lounge." This sets a specific condition for entry.

Incorrect Choices:

- Choice B is not mentioned.
- Choice C is incorrect because the lounge allows "refreshments," while the ban on water applies to the labs.
- Choice D is contradicted by the statement that it is a "24-hour study area."

When you hear the word "However," get ready to take notes! In TOEFL announcements, "However" usually marks the transition from a restriction (no food in labs) to an allowance or exception (food is okay in the lounge). Questions frequently target this specific exception because it requires the listener to follow the logic of the entire message.

Question 9:

Correct Choice:

- Choice C: The announcement explicitly states that the Blue Line will be suspended due to roadwork.

Incorrect Choices:

- Choice A is incorrect because the Gold Line is being *rerouted*, not replaced.
- Choice B is incorrect because the Blue Line isn't running at all.
- Choice D is a common "over-generalization" distractor; only the Blue Line is suspended, while the Gold Line remains active.

Question 10:

Correct Choice:

- Choice B: At the end of the announcement, the speaker tells students to "consult the 'Campus Transit' mobile app" for real-time updates.

Incorrect Choices:

- Choice A is not mentioned as a suggestion.
- Choice C confuses the "stop" at the Health Center with a suggestion for parking.
- Choice D is incorrect because the speaker suggests allowing extra time in the *morning*, not avoiding the bus in the afternoon.

In announcements regarding schedules or routes, listen for specific colors, numbers, or names. The test-makers often mention two different things (like the Blue Line and the Gold Line) to see if you can keep track of which one is changing and which one is staying the same. Taking a quick note like "Blue = Stop" and "Gold = Reroute" can save you from getting these confused!

Question 11:

Correct Choice:

- Choice B: The lecture explains what the Silk Road was (a trade network) and why it mattered (it moved goods and ideas).

Incorrect Choices:

- Choice A is too narrow.
- Choices C and D are not mentioned.

Question 12:

Correct Choice:

- Choice B: The professor states that "China was the only place in the world that knew how to make silk," which made it highly desired by others.

Incorrect Choices:

- Choice A is incorrect because while silk was very valuable (like money), the professor never says it was actually *used* as currency. This is a "common sense" distractor—it sounds like it might be true in history, but it wasn't mentioned in the talk.
- Choice C was used to make paper and gunpowder. This choice mixes up different details. Paper and gunpowder were mentioned as *other* inventions shared on the road, but they have nothing to do with the physical material of silk.
- Choice D is the exact opposite of what the professor said. He mentioned it was "very expensive" and that only one country knew the secret to making it.

Question 13:

Correct Choice:

- Choice B: The term "cultural bridge" refers to the exchange of nonphysical things. The professor gives the example of Buddhism (a religion) and papermaking (an invention) moving between countries.

Incorrect Choices:

- Choice A is a "literal trap." The professor is using a metaphor (a "bridge" for ideas). In academic talks, if a term sounds too strange to be literal (a bridge made of fabric?), it is almost certainly a figure of speech.
- Choice C, the professor mentions "inventions," which might make you think of "builders" or "design," but the lecture never discusses urban planning or city construction.
- Choice D uses modern logic. While people did travel, they traveled for trade and religion, not for "vacations." This is a "misplaced concept" distractor.

Question 14:

Correct Choice:

- Choice C: The professor lists "silk, spices, and tea" as goods carried by traders. Spices is the only one of those three listed in the options.

Incorrect Choices:

- Choice A, the professor mentions Rome, but he says Romans *bought* the silk; he never mentions them sending statues back to China.
- Choice B is a "related category" distractor. Cotton is a fabric like silk, but it was not mentioned in the talk. The test is checking to see if you can remember the specific list (silk, spices, tea).
- Choice D while coins were likely used to buy the silk, they were not one of the specific goods listed by the professor as items carried along the network.

When you see an incorrect answer that uses a word you definitely heard (like "Rome" or "Paper"), stop and ask: "Did the professor connect these two words in the way the answer choice does?" The exam could take two true words and create a false relationship between them.

Question 15:

Correct Choice:

- Choice B: The professor defines the "Urban Heat Island effect" and explains the science behind why cities are warmer.

Incorrect Choices:

- Choice A is incorrect because the talk isn't about plant growth rates.
- Choice C is incorrect because while asphalt and brick are mentioned, the talk isn't about construction techniques.
- Choice D is incorrect because air conditioning is mentioned as a result of the heat, not the main topic of the history lesson.

Question 16:

Correct Choice:

- Choice C: The professor states these materials "absorb and trap heat" and "slowly release that heat back into the air."

Incorrect Choices:

- Choice A is incorrect because the talk says they *absorb* heat, not reflect light.
- Choice B is incorrect because the cost of repairs is never discussed.
- Choice D is true in reality, but this specific detail was not mentioned in the talk.

Question 17:

Correct Choice:

- Choice C: The professor states they "help to lower the temperature of the entire building."

Incorrect Choices:

- Choice A, while green roofs *can* grow food, the professor specifically focuses on their role as a "natural cooling system."
- Choice B is incorrect. Appearance/aesthetics are not mentioned.
- Choice D is incorrect. The professor doesn't compare the difficulty of building different roof types.

Question 18:

Correct Choice:

- Choice C: The professor says the heat "increases the demand for air conditioning," implying that people must use it more because the city is so hot.

Incorrect Choices:

- Choice A incorrect. Air conditioning is a *response* to the heat, while the building materials are the *cause*.
- Choice B, there is no comparison made to the cost of electricity in the country.
- Choice D is incorrect because the professor suggests green roofs "help," but never says they will "entirely replace" air conditioning.

In academic science talks, listen for **comparisons**. The professor compares "Rural Areas" (greenery, shade, cool) to "Urban Areas" (asphalt, trapped heat, warm). Often, a question will ask you to identify a specific characteristic of one side of that comparison.

CHAPTER 4

Writing

In the Writing section of the TOEFL iBT, you will see 12 items in total, appearing in three different types of tasks. The three question types are called a Build a Sentence, Write an Email, and Write for an Academic Discussion. We will go over each of these question types in depth in this chapter and share some helpful strategies along the way. At the end of the chapter are more practice questions followed by their answers and explanations.

Question Type: Build a Sentence

The *Build a Sentence* task is designed to test your skills of recognizing and manipulating sentence structures. To a lesser extent, the *Build a Sentence* task tests your grammar skills.

You will see two sentences on the screen. The first sentence will be complete. The second sentence will have words or phrases in the wrong order. You have to move the words and phrases around in the second sentence in order to form a grammatically correct sentence. The two sentences taken together form an exchange between two speakers, so the sentence that you create must not only be grammatically correct, but also must constitute an appropriate reply to the first sentence.

The skills tested in the *Build a Sentence* tasks are crucial for daily life. Practicing with these will not only help your score on the TOEFL iBT, but also will help you become a better communicator!

Here is an example:

> "Have you decided which elective course you're going to take next semester?"
>
> "I ___ ___ ___ ___ ___ ___ ___ ___ ___ history."
>
> narrowed down options to has was art either or have my

When you approach a *Build a Sentence* task, **first read the initial sentence carefully**. Before you even look at the second sentence and word bank below, try to imagine what ideas might be expressed in possible replies. Your goal with this step is to force yourself to focus on the context so that your mind is primed to put together an appropriate reply to the first sentence. Remember, the two sentences together are supposed to represent an exchange between speakers.

In our example, the first speaker is asking whether the second speaker has *decided* something, in particular which elective course to take next semester.

You now know what the second sentence must address, and you can imagine replies such as "Yes, I'm taking course X," or "No, I'm still trying to decide." Obviously, there are many appropriate replies, but at least now your mind won't consider the second sentence as an independent puzzle to figure out. You will naturally attempt to create an appropriate response to the first sentence.

Next, **look at the words that already appear in the second sentence**. There might be as few as two words, but that can still be helpful. In our sample, we see that the sentence ends with *history*. Is the second speaker replying that they decided to take a course in history? We're not sure at this point, and we don't want to spend much time here, but this adds one more clue to help us when we look at the word bank below the question.

Now **look at the word bank**. Keep in mind that some questions might be designed so that you will use all of the words in the word bank, while others will have an extra word or two that will not appear in the final sentence. This makes the task a bit more challenging and tests your ability to select the words that will make the sentence grammatically correct.

Scan the words in the word bank and **look for verbs**. These are the action words. In our sample question, we see the verb *narrowed*. We also see the helping verbs *has*, *have*, and *was*, but active verbs like *narrowed* will be most useful at first. When discussing a decision, to *narrow* means to limit the choices being considered. Just from this verb we can now know that the second speaker hasn't decided on one particular class yet, including history.

Now **check the word bank for grammatical pairs**. If you see "not only," look for "but also." If you see "neither," look for "nor." These pairs act as "anchors" that help you snap the rest of the sentence into place. In our sample question, we have *either* and *or*, which fits in well with the idea of narrowing a decision down to two possibilities. While scanning the word bank, you might have also noticed another word that supports this: *options*.

At this point you can determine that the speaker has narrowed their decision down to two options, one of them being history. Look at the word bank to see that the other course the speaker might be considering is *art*.

At this point you are ready to **start placing the words**. Match the proper verb forms and use proper grammar. The first speaker asked, "Have you decided . . . ," so an appropriate reply would use the verb form, "have narrowed." Place those words and go from there.

Correct Answer: I have narrowed down my options to either art or history.

Note that this example contained two unused words as distractors:

has: Incorrect subject-verb agreement (should be "I have," not "I has").
was: Changes the tense to a passive or past progressive structure that doesn't fit the phrasal verb "narrowed down" in this context.

Question Type: Write an Email

As the name indicates, the *Write an Email* task will require you to compose an email. It will present you with a written description of a scenario in an academic or social situation. It will then describe to you the purpose of your email. You might, for example, be composing the email in order to extend an invitation, or request more information, or recommend something, or try to solve a problem. You will then have 7 minutes to compose the email.

The *Write an Email* task is designed to measure your ability to create a multisentence written text that not only uses correct English spelling, punctuation, capitalization, and a variety of grammar structures and vocabulary, but that is also clear enough, sufficiently in-depth, follows basic social conventions, and achieves the stated goals.

As a TOEFL student, you will certainly have to write a number of emails in English. Practicing with the *Write an Email* task will not only help you achieve a higher score on the TOEFL iBT but also will help you build important real-life skills.

Here is a practice example:

You are a university student planning to apply for a competitive summer internship in environmental research. To complete your application, you need a letter of recommendation from a professor who knows your work well. You have decided to email Dr. Aris, your biology professor from last semester, whose class you really enjoyed and excelled in.

Write an email to Dr. Aris requesting a letter of recommendation. In your email, you should do the following:

- State clearly why you are writing to her.
- Briefly remind her who you are and mention a specific project or achievement from her class.
- Explain why you believe she is the best person to recommend you for this specific internship.

Answer/Explanation:

A potential email could be:

Subject: Letter of Recommendation Request

Dear Dr. Aris,

I hope you are having a productive semester. I am writing to you because I am currently applying for a summer internship at the Coastal Research Institute, and I was hoping you might be willing to write a letter of recommendation on my behalf.

I was a student in your "Marine Ecosystems" course last fall. I particularly enjoyed working on the final lab report regarding local water quality, which received an 'A' and inspired me to pursue further research in this field.

Since this internship focuses heavily on the conservation topics we covered in your lectures, I believe your perspective on my academic performance and lab skills would be invaluable to my application.

Thank you for your time and for considering my request. I look forward to hearing from you.

Sincerely,

[Your Name]

This email works well because it meets the following criteria, which you should also use whenever you do a Write an Email task:

- **Goal Alignment**: It hits all three bullet points. It states the purpose immediately, references the "Marine Ecosystems" course/lab report, and connects the professor's expertise to the specific internship. *It's crucial that your email address all of the bullet points.* This is one of the most important strategies to keep in mind when crafting your response.

- **Tone and Etiquette**: This uses a formal register ("Dear Dr. Aris," "Sincerely," "invaluable"). This is appropriate for a student-to-professor interaction. Other types of emails might require a different tone. For example, if you are writing to fellow students in order to invite them to join a club, your tone would be more casual, following the social conventions for such an email. *Pay attention to your audience* and the email's purpose and choose your tone and social conventions accordingly.
- **Sufficiently In-Depth:** There is nothing missing from this email. The professor has everything they need to answer it appropriately. Notice how the email includes specific details about the course and the work the student did. You must always provide enough detail to make sure the email is sufficiently in-depth. Of course, you will have to make up such details. Don't be shy. This is expected and without such detail your email will appear incomplete. At the same time, notice how this email gets straight to the point, which is essential for a 7-minute task. You won't get extra points for long-winded emails. Provide enough detail, but do it in a clear and concise manner.
- **Grammar, Spelling, and Variety**: The email is grammatically correct. There are no glaring spelling errors and the email uses a varied vocabulary. It uses complex structures like "I was hoping you might be willing" and "Since this internship focuses . . . I believe . . ." to show advanced English proficiency.

Question Type: Writing for an Academic Discussion

For this task, the on-screen interface is designed to resemble an online academic discussion between a professor and their class. The professor will give some background and then pose a question to the class in which you are supposedly a student. You will see a couple of responses to the professor's question, posted by other students in the class. There will be an area where you will type your own response. You will have 10 minutes to complete the task.

This task is designed to evaluate your ability to contribute to a typical academic discussion, to develop and support your ideas while using correct word choices, spelling, punctuation, grammar, and vocabulary. An effective response will contain at least 100 words, though the length of your response is not something the graders are specifically looking at.

The grading is not looking for perfection. It is understood that even good writers make mistakes when they are under time pressure. That being said, they will look for three things in your response:

- **Relevant and clearly developed ideas**. This relates to how well you support your ideas with reasons and examples and how relevant your ideas are to the discussion.
- **Variety in the use of language**. This relates to the vocabulary and structures that you use in your response.
- **Correct use of language**. Graders want to see that your word choices are correct and appropriate, that you use correct spelling, punctuation, and capitalization, and that your use of grammar is strong and consistent.

Here is a practice example:

Instructions: Your professor is teaching a class on Urban Planning. Write a post responding to the professor's question. In your response, you should do the following:

- Express and support your opinion.
- Make a contribution to the discussion in your own words.
- An effective response will contain at least 100 words.

[Professor Jordan] Next week, we will look at how city layouts affect public health and the environment. Specifically, many modern cities are moving toward "pedestrian-only" zones, which are areas where cars are completely banned from the city center to encourage walking, cycling, and the use of public transit. Supporters argue this significantly reduces air pollution and makes cities safer and more vibrant. Opponents, however, point out that these bans can hurt local businesses that rely on deliveries and car-commuting customers, and may make commuting much harder for people living in the suburbs. In your opinion, should city governments prioritize creating more car-free zones in their downtown areas?

[Kelly] I'm all for it! Car-free zones make the city much more livable. When you remove cars, you get less noise and cleaner air. It also encourages people to exercise more by walking between shops or offices. Plus, these areas usually become popular social hubs with outdoor seating and street performers, which is great for the community spirit.

[Andrew] I think it's a risky move. Many people don't have the luxury of living near a subway station, so they have to drive to work. If you ban cars, you're essentially telling those people they aren't welcome downtown. Also, think about small businesses—if customers can't find easy parking nearby, they'll just stay in the suburbs and shop at big malls instead. This could end up killing the "vibrant" city centers we're trying to save.

[Your Response]:

Answer/Explanation:

A potential response could be:

In my opinion, it's a great idea to prioritize creating more car-free zones in downtown areas. It not only improves air quality, as Kelly said, but it reclaims public space for people rather than machinery. Anyone who has walked around a car-free zone knows that it's a much more inviting and pleasant environment. It's also safer, as Professor Jordan noted. Although Andrew raises valid concerns regarding accessibility, there's a way to deal with this. The city can simultaneously invest in "park-and-ride" facilities on the outskirts of the city. This would allow suburban commuters to park their vehicles easily and take a quick shuttle or light rail into the pedestrian center. By doing this, the city maintains its business revenue without the congestion of individual cars. If they do this, then car-free zones can be a win for everyone.

Why this response would score highly:

- The ideas are relevant and clearly expressed: It establishes a clear opinion, supports it with multiple reasons, and introduces a new solution ("park-and-ride" facilities).
- It demonstrates variety in the use of language. It uses some precise word choices, such as "reclaims" and "valid concerns." It uses some complex sentence structure, including "not only . . . but it also . . ."
- The language is strong, consistent, and grammatically precise.

How to Approach the Writing for an Academic Discussion Task

1. Read the professor's post and summarize the question.

Because of the time pressure, test takers sometimes make the mistake of merely skimming through the professor's post. They feel pulled toward the other students' posts and spend more time reading those in order to satisfy the urge to "know what everyone else is doing." This is a bad idea, because it's crucial that you fully understand both the background information that the professor provides and the specific question that the professor asks. So, don't rush here, and don't even look at the other students' posts until you are sure that you are clear about what the professor is asking.

2. Brainstorm.

Imagine you weren't taking the TOEFL iBT exam, but were actually chatting with your professor and class. Forget how you would express your post in English for now. At first, just think about what you would actually like to convey to the professor and fellow students. What would you truly like to say in order to contribute to the conversation? Let the question sink in, and let your mind generate ideas. Don't judge the ideas; just let them flow. If you find that there is one clear answer that is "calling you," and you cannot come up with any more, then move on. You just want to make sure you are giving yourself enough time to generate ideas.

3. Choose your ideas and prepare your response.

Before deciding on what to write about, take a look at what the other students have written (if you haven't already). It's fine if there is a bit of overlap between what another student wrote and what you want to write, but you have to avoid saying basically the same thing as another student. Don't dwell on the other students' posts. You are not trying to learn anything from them besides the topics the other students wrote about. You can refer to the other students' posts in your own response, but don't make your post all about agreeing or disagreeing with another student. Develop your own contribution to the discussion.

4. Write an organized response.

Even though the online discussion format makes this task somewhat informal, you should still aim to write an organized response.

Your first sentence should introduce your opinion. Be professional, but personable. Here are some ways you might begin your post:

For me . . .

In my opinion . . .

My classmates make great points. In my opinion . . .

The other responses are interesting, but for me . . .

It seems to me that . . .

Then, give your first reason and discuss it. Develop it. If you have a second reason, move on to it and support that reason. Finish off with a concluding sentence.

Although you are creating an organized post, you don't want to sound too formal. This is not an essay, but rather a post in an online discussion. You probably wouldn't want to connect your ideas with very formal transition words such as "moreover" or "hence," because that's not typical for such a forum. Instead of "moreover," you might say "also." Instead of "hence," you would probably say "so." Use your own words and phrases the way you naturally would.

5. Edit before you submit.

As you probably would if you were truly participating in an online discussion with your professor and classmates, take a moment before submitting to check what you wrote.

Timing on the Writing for an Academic Discussion Task

You only have 10 minutes total. All of your prep work (Steps 1–3 above) should take no more than 2 minutes. Then, write for 7 minutes. If you have done Steps 1–3 properly, this should be quite reasonable. Leave 1 minute at the end to proofread and edit.

General Strategies

Success on the TOEFL iBT Writing section is about predictability and precision. Because you are under a tight clock (especially in the 7-minute and 10-minute tasks), you don't have time to be a "creative" writer. Instead, you need to be a "structured" writer.

Here are the essential strategies to help you dominate the writing portion:

1. Master the "Template" Mindset

   Don't reinvent the wheel every time you start a task. Have a mental skeleton ready for each response type.

- For Write an Email:
  - *Salutation:* "Dear [Name],"
  - *Context:* "I am writing to you regarding . . ."
  - *Call to Action:* "Could you please let me know if . . ."
- For Academic Discussion:
  - *Opening:* "In my opinion, [Student Name] makes a valid point, but I believe . . ."
  - *Body:* "One factor that hasn't been mentioned is [Your New Idea] . . ."
  - *Closing:* "Ultimately, this approach ensures that . . ."

2. Use "Signpost" Transitions

   Transitions are great because they make your logic easy to follow. They act like a map for the reader.

TO ADD INFORMATION	TO SHOW CONTRAST	TO SHOW CAUSE/EFFECT
Furthermore	However	Consequently
Additionally	On the other hand	Therefore
Moreover	Conversely	As a result

3. The "1-Minute Polish" Rule

   Never write until the very last second. In a 7 or 10-minute task, your brain is moving faster than your fingers, which leads to "typo" errors (e.g., writing "they was" instead of "they were").

- Strategy: Stop typing when there is 60 seconds left.
- Check for: Subject-verb agreement, plural "s" on nouns, and capital letters at the start of sentences. These small fixes can jump your score.

4. Address the "Implicit" Audience

   Each task has a specific audience. Your score depends on hitting the right register:

- Professor: Use formal, academic vocabulary (*inquire, prioritize, objective*).
- Peer/Teammate: Use semiformal, polite language (*reach out, check in, looking forward to*).
- Public/General: Use clear, persuasive language that weighs different sides of an issue.

5. Development Over Length

   While the Academic Discussion asks for 100 words, 200 words of "fluff" (repeating the same idea over and over) is worse than 120 words of high-quality, distinct ideas.

6. Ask Yourself: "Did I provide a specific example?"

   Instead of: "Technology is good for students," try, "Technology, such as interactive simulation software, allows biology students to visualize complex cellular processes that are invisible to the naked eye."

More Practice

Question 1: Build a Sentence

The university library is closing for renovations next week, isn't it?

Yes, ___ ___ ___ ___ ___ ___ ___ ___ students.

it be closed to is renovations during months all will for

Question 2: Build a Sentence

I heard the professor changed the deadline for our final research paper.

Correct, ___ ___ ___ ___ ___ ___ ___ ___ ___ Monday.

has to the deadline until next was is she extend decided

Question 3: Build a Sentence

I'm having trouble finding the sources I need for my sociology presentation.

You should ___ ___ ___ ___ ___ ___ ___ ___ assistance.

ask the to for librarian by at desk help reference a

Question 4: Build a Sentence

I'm really struggling with the advanced calculus formulas we covered in class today.

You ___ ___ ___ ___ ___ ___ ___ session.

for tutoring sign up a in with private the could

Question 5: Write an Email

You are working on a group project for your Marketing class. One of your teammates, Sarah, has missed the last two group meetings and has not responded to the messages sent in your group chat. The final presentation is due in four days, and Sarah is responsible for a significant portion of the data analysis.

Task: Write an email to Sarah to address the situation. In your email, you should do the following:

- Inquire if she is doing okay and mention her recent absences.
- Explain the current status of the project and the approaching deadline.
- Suggest a specific way or time for her to check in and share her progress.

Question 6: Write an Email

You are the president of the University Hiking Club. You are planning a group excursion to a national park next Saturday, but the club's usual transport van is currently being repaired. You need to email the Campus Transportation Office to see if it is possible to reserve an alternative vehicle.

Task: Write an email to the Transportation Coordinator. In your email, you should do the following:

- Explain who you are and why you are contacting the office.
- Provide the specific details of your trip (date and number of participants).
- Ask about the availability of an alternative vehicle and the process for reserving it.

Question 7: Writing for an Academic Discussion

Instructions: Your professor is teaching a class on Education. Write a post responding to the professor's question. In your response, you should do the following:

- Express and support your opinion.
- Make a contribution to the discussion in your own words.
- An effective response will contain at least 100 words.

[Professor Henderson] This week we're discussing the allocation of limited resources in public schools. Many school districts are facing budget cuts and must choose between maintaining traditional academic programs or continuing to fund "extracurricular" activities, such as competitive sports, music, and drama programs. Some argue that these activities are essential for a well-rounded education and student engagement. Others believe that when funds are low, the priority must be strictly on core academic subjects like math, science, and literacy. If you were a school board member, would you support cutting funding for extracurricular activities to protect academic programs? Why or why not?

[Rachel] I think we have to protect the core academics first. The primary goal of a school is to ensure that students are literate and proficient in STEM subjects so they can succeed in the workforce. While sports and music are "nice to have," they aren't strictly necessary for a student's future career in the same way that math or writing skills are. We shouldn't compromise the quality of basic education just to keep a football team.

[David] I disagree with Rachel. For many students, extracurriculars are the only reason they stay motivated to come to school at all. These programs teach teamwork, discipline, and time management in ways a math textbook never could. If you cut the arts and sports, you'll likely see a drop in overall student attendance and engagement, which will eventually hurt their academic performance anyway.

[Your Response]:

Question 8: Writing for an Academic Discussion

Instructions: Your professor is teaching a class on Business Ethics. Write a post responding to the professor's question. In your response, you should do the following:

- Express and support your opinion.
- Make a contribution to the discussion in your own words.
- An effective response will contain at least 100 words.

[Professor Miller] We've been discussing "Corporate Social Responsibility." Recently, several major international corporations have announced that they will no longer use plastic packaging for their products, opting instead for more expensive biodegradable materials. While this is clearly better for the environment, it often results in higher prices for the average consumer. Some people argue that corporations have an ethical obligation to protect the planet regardless of the cost. Others contend that in a difficult economy, a company's primary responsibility is to keep their products affordable for the public. What is your take? Should companies prioritize environmental sustainability even if it significantly raises the cost of essential goods?

[Sarah] I believe the environment must come first. We are facing a global climate crisis, and the long-term cost of pollution is much higher than a small increase in the price of a bottle of shampoo. If large corporations don't lead the way, change will never happen. Consumers will eventually adjust their spending habits, and the planet will benefit in the long run.

[James] I have to disagree. It's easy to say "the environment first" if you have a high income, but for many families, every dollar counts. If essential items like soap, food, or cleaning supplies become more expensive because of fancy packaging, it's the lower-income population that suffers most. Companies should find ways to be green without passing the entire financial burden onto people who are already struggling to get by.

[Your Response]:

Answers and Explanations

Question 1:

"Yes, it will be closed during renovations for all students."

1. Grammar (Future Passive/Adjective): The structure "it will be closed" correctly uses the future tense to describe a state that hasn't happened yet but is scheduled.
2. Distractors (Unused Words):
   - "is": This is a "tense trap." While "It is closed" is grammatically correct, it contradicts the context of "next week" provided by Speaker 1.
   - "to": This is simply an extra word not needed.
   - "months": This describes a time period, which makes sense, but it doesn't fit this set of words and number of blanks.

Tips for This Task:

- Look for the "Anchor": Identify the subject (it) and the verb (will be closed) first.
- Check the Ending: Always look at the word provided after the blanks (in this case, "students"). This tells you that the word immediately before it must be a modifier or part of a prepositional phrase (like "all students" or "to students").
- Tense Agreement: Always match the timeframe of Speaker 1. If they say "next week," avoid using "is" or "was."

Question 2:

"Correct, she has decided to extend the deadline until next Monday."

1. Grammar (Present Perfect): The sentence uses the present perfect tense ("she has decided") to describe a recent action that affects the present situation (the new deadline).
2. Infinitive Phrase: The structure "decided to extend" tests the ability to link a main verb with an infinitive object.
3. Contextual Logic: The word "until" is the correct preposition to use when discussing a time limit or a deadline extension.
4. Distractors (Unused Words):
   - "was" and "is": These are auxiliary verbs that do not fit the "has decided" structure. Using "she was decided" or "she is decided" is grammatically incorrect in this active context.

TOEFL Tip: When you see a bank of words, try to group them into "chunks" first (e.g., "the deadline," "decided to," "until next"). This makes it much easier to assemble the final sequence!

Question 3:

"You should ask a librarian at the reference desk for assistance."

1. Verb Patterns: The verb "ask" has two common patterns. You can *ask a question* or *ask [someone] for [something]*. In this case, the student is asking a person (librarian) for a thing (assistance).
2. Noun Adjuncts: "Reference desk" is a compound noun. In English, we often use one noun to describe another. Identifying these pairs helps you realize that "reference" and "desk" must stay together.
3. Distractor Strategy:
   - "To" is a distractor because "ask" does not require "to" before the object (you don't "ask to a librarian").
   - "By" is a distractor because while you can be *by* a desk, the standard idiomatic expression for a service station is being *at* the desk.

Question 4:

"You could sign up for a private tutoring session."

TOEFL Tip: "Sign up" is a common phrasal verb. This example separates the verb ("sign") and the particle ("up") in the word bank to see if you can link them.

Question 5:

A potential email could be:

> Subject: Following up on our Marketing project
>
> Hi Sarah,
>
> I hope everything is going well with you. I'm reaching out because the rest of the group noticed you weren't able to make it to our last two meetings, and we haven't heard from you in the chat. We wanted to check in and make sure you're okay.
>
> As you know, our final presentation is due this Friday. We have most of the slides ready, but we are still missing the data analysis section that you are working on. We really need to integrate that data soon so we can practice the full presentation together.
>
> Could you please give us an update by tomorrow morning? If you're having trouble finishing your part, let us know so we can all figure out a solution together before the deadline.
>
> Best,
>
> [Your Name]

Why this email works:

- Social Conventions: The email starts with a friendly "I hope everything is going well," which is a standard social convention when addressing a missing peer. It avoids sounding overly aggressive while still being professional.
- Clarity of Goals: 1. It addresses the absences and asks if she is okay. 2. It mentions the Friday deadline and the specific missing section (data analysis). 3. It sets a clear expectation ("update by tomorrow morning").
- Vocabulary & Grammar: The response uses an effective transitional phrase like "As you know" and utilizes the present continuous tense ("you are working on," "we are still missing") to describe the current state of the project.
- Register: The tone is semiformal. Since Sarah is a peer, "Hi Sarah" and "Best" are appropriate, but the body of the email remains focused and serious because of the looming deadline.

Pro-Tip: In "problem-solving" emails like this, the key is to be constructive. Instead of just complaining, the writer offers a way forward (asking for an update by a specific time), which shows the "in-depth" communication skills.

Question 6:

A potential email could be:

Subject: Urgent Vehicle Reservation Request – Hiking Club

Dear Transportation Coordinator,

My name is [Your Name], and I am the president of the University Hiking Club. I am writing to inquire about the possibility of renting a campus vehicle for an upcoming club event.

We have a group excursion scheduled for next Saturday, October 14th. We expect to have 12 students participating in the trip, but unfortunately, our primary club van is currently in the shop for repairs.

Could you please let me know if there is a passenger van available for that date? Additionally, if a vehicle is free, please clarify what specific forms or authorizations we need to submit to finalize the reservation.

Thank you for your assistance with this matter.

Best regards,

[Your Name] President, University Hiking Club

Why this email works:

- Structure & Hierarchy: The email uses a clear subject line and formal sign-off, which is essential when communicating with university staff.
- Specific Details: By including the date (Oct 14th) and the number of people (12), the writer fulfills the "sufficiently in-depth" requirement. Without these details, the Transportation Office wouldn't be able to help.
- Tone: It is professional and respectful, using phrases like "inquire about" and "assistance with this matter" rather than "I want" or "Help me."

TOEFL Writing Tip:

When you have 7 minutes, spend the first 1 minute "mentally mapping" your three bullet points. Spend 5 minutes writing, and use the final minute to check your verb tenses (e.g., ensuring you used "scheduled" for the future event and "is" for the current repair).

Question 7:

A potential response could be:

In my view, while Rachel makes a practical point regarding the necessity of core literacy and STEM proficiency, I find myself agreeing more with David's holistic view of education. However, I would like to propose a middle-ground perspective that hasn't been mentioned yet: the role of community partnerships.

Rather than viewing this as a binary choice between "cutting" or "keeping" programs, school boards should look into collaborating with local non-profits or private businesses to co-fund these activities. For instance, a local tech company might sponsor a robotics club, or a community conservatory might provide music instruction. This approach protects the school's budget for core subjects while ensuring that the "soft skills" David mentioned—like teamwork and discipline—remain part of the curriculum. Ultimately, a school that only teaches from a textbook fails to prepare students for the social complexities of the real world, so we must find creative ways to keep these programs alive.

Why this response would score highly:

- Critically Engaged: It summarizes the two existing viewpoints ("practical point" vs. "holistic view") and then pivots to a new idea.
- Original Contribution: It introduces the concept of "community partnerships" or "private sponsorship," which shows the ability to think critically about the prompt rather than just picking a side.
- Transitional Phrases: Uses sophisticated connectors like *Rather than, For instance, In my view*, and *Ultimately*.
- Vocabulary: Uses high-level terms such as *allocation, proficiency, holistic, binary choice*, and *curriculum*.
- Tone: The tone is academic and persuasive, perfect for a university-level discussion board.

Quick Tips for your 10-minute countdown:

1. Acknowledge: Spend the first sentence briefly mentioning what Rachel or David said.
2. Add: Spend the next three or four sentences explaining your specific "why" or a new "how."
3. Conclude: End with a strong "big picture" statement about the importance of the topic.

Question 8:

A potential response could be:

> While Sarah and James both make compelling points regarding the tension between ethics and economics, I believe the responsibility should not rest solely on the company or the consumer. In my view, the most effective way to resolve this issue is through government intervention in the form of subsidies.
>
> If a corporation decides to switch to eco-friendly, biodegradable packaging, the government should provide tax incentives or grants to offset the increased production costs. This would allow the company to fulfill its ethical duty to the environment—as Sarah suggests—without forcing James's concerned low-income consumers to pay higher prices. Furthermore, this approach encourages innovation; when green materials are subsidized, they eventually become cheaper than plastic due to increased demand and mass production. Ultimately, we cannot expect the "free market" alone to solve an environmental crisis; it requires a collaborative effort between the public and private sectors to ensure that sustainability remains affordable for everyone.

Why this response would score highly:

- The "Middle Way" Strategy: Instead of just agreeing with Sarah or James, the writer introduces a third party (the government). This shows high-level critical thinking and "academic maturity."
- Vocabulary & Phrasing: Uses sophisticated language like *compelling points, solely, government intervention, tax incentives*, and *collaborative effort*.
- Logical Flow: The response transitions smoothly from acknowledging the previous speakers to presenting a solution, and then explaining the long-term benefits of that solution.
- Grammar Precision: The writer uses the conditional mood correctly ("This would allow . . .") to discuss a hypothetical policy, which is a hallmark of advanced English proficiency.

Practice Tip:

When you are taking the actual test, try to use "voice" words. These are words that show you are participating in a conversation, such as:

- *"To build on Sarah's point . . ."*
- *"While I understand James's concern about . . ."*
- *"A perspective that hasn't been fully explored yet is . . ."*

These phrases immediately signal to the grader that you are fulfilling the "contribution to the discussion" requirement!

CHAPTER 5

Speaking

In the Speaking section of the TOEFL iBT, you will see 11 items in total, appearing in two different overall tasks. The two tasks are called Listen and Repeat and Take an Interview. We will go over these question types/tasks in depth in this chapter and share some helpful strategies along the way. At the end of the chapter are more practice questions followed by their answers and explanations.

Question Type: Listen and Repeat

With the *Listen and Repeat* task, you will see a visual representation of some academic or campus life setting which forms the background for a scenario. You must listen to and then repeat seven sentences relating to the scenario, one at a time. You will have a maximum of 8 to 12 seconds to process the sentence you heard and then to repeat the sentence out loud. The time varies because the sentences get progressively longer and more complex as you progress through the scenario.

The purpose of this task is to test both your ability to process the sentences you hear and to accurately and intelligibly reproduce those sentences. This serves as a measure of foundational language skills such as the ability to process language and produce fluent and intelligible speech.

Here is an example:

*Listen to **Audio File #13** in your online companion.*

The Audio (What you will see and hear online):

Scenario Context: A university student is visiting the campus Career Services Center for the first time.

Visual Setting: An office with desks, stacks of brochures, and a large bulletin board labeled "Internships."

Narrator: You are visiting the Career Services Center on campus. Listen to the counselor and repeat what he says. You will have a set amount of time after each sentence to repeat it exactly.

Man: We offer several resources for career planning.
(pause for 8–12 seconds for you to repeat)

Man: You can schedule a meeting with an advisor online.
(pause for 8–12 seconds for you to repeat)

Man: If you have a draft of your resume, I can look at it now.
(pause for 8–12 seconds for you to repeat)

Man: Most students find that a mock interview helps reduce their anxiety before the real thing.
(pause for 8–12 seconds for you to repeat)

Man: Our database contains hundreds of local internship opportunities specifically curated for undergraduate students.
(pause for 8–12 seconds for you to repeat)

Man: Please remember that you must register at least 48 hours in advance for the upcoming job fair.
(pause for 8–12 seconds for you to repeat)

Man: Although most workshops are held in this building, the networking seminar on Friday has been moved to the student union.
(pause for 8–12 seconds for you to repeat)

Answer Key and Explanation

SEQUENCE	FULL SENTENCE	LINGUISTIC FOCUS & COMMON PITFALLS
1	We offer several resources for career planning.	Word Stress: Ensure "re-SOURCES" and "ca-REER" are stressed correctly.
2	You can schedule a meeting with an advisor online.	Function Words: Don't drop the "an" before "advisor."
3	If you have a draft of your resume, I can look at it now.	Conditional Phrasing: Maintain the rising intonation at the comma.
4	Most students find that a mock interview helps reduce their anxiety before the real thing.	Noun Phrases: "Mock interview" and "real thing" should be spoken as cohesive units.
5	Our database contains hundreds of local internship opportunities specifically curated for undergraduate students.	Academic Vocabulary: "Curated" and "Undergraduate" test your ability to handle multisyllabic words under pressure.
6	Please remember that you must register at least 48 hours in advance for the upcoming job fair.	Numbers & Prepositions: "48 hours" and "in advance" are key technical details that must be exact.
7	Although most workshops are held in this building, the networking seminar on Friday has been moved to the student union.	Complex Transition: "Although" sets up a contrast; ensure the second half of the sentence resolves the thought clearly.

Pro-Tips for Success

- **Don't Paraphrase:** Unlike other Speaking tasks, this is a test of **reproduction**. Even if "job fair" and "career expo" mean the same thing, using the wrong word will lower your score.
- **Focus on "Chunks":** As the sentences get longer (like Sentence 7), try to hear them in groups of words (e.g., *[Although most workshops] [are held in this building]* . . .). It is easier to remember three "chunks" than fifteen individual words.
- **Keep the Pace:** If you stumble on a word, don't stop. Keep going to maintain the "flow" and "intelligibility" of the remaining sentence.

Question Type: Take an Interview

In the *Take an Interview* task, you will answer four questions in a simulated conversation with a prerecorded interviewer. The interview supposedly takes place as part of a research study, an application for a scholarship, or other similar situation. The early questions will focus on factual information and your own personal experiences. The latter questions will require you to give your opinions about broader issues and then support those opinions. You are always given 45 seconds to answer each question.

The purpose of this task is to measure your ability to communicate by having you speak about your opinions and experiences in the context of a simulated conversation. More specifically, the test maker is looking for spoken responses that are coherent, answer the question, keep a steady, conversational speaking pace, are easy to understand, use rhythm and intonation to convey meaning, and use a range of vocabulary and grammatical structures.

Here is an example:

*Listen to **Audio File #16** in your online companion.*

The Audio (What you will hear online):

Narrator: You are participating in a research study about how modern work environments affect productivity and work-life balance. You have agreed to a short online interview. The researcher will now ask you four questions.

Interviewer: Hi there! Thank you for participating in our study. To start, could you tell me about a time you had to complete a project or a difficult task? Where did you choose to work—was it a library, a quiet office, or maybe a busy cafe? Why did you pick that specific location?
(pause for 45-second response)

Interviewer: That's interesting. People often have strong preferences regarding their surroundings. Some people feel they are most productive when they are entirely alone in a silent room, while others prefer having some background noise or people around them. Which environment do you prefer when you really need to focus, and why does that work for you?
(pause for 45-second response)

Interviewer: Excellent. Now, let's look at a broader trend. Many companies are now allowing employees to work from home permanently. Proponents argue this increases job satisfaction and saves time. However, others claim that working in a shared physical office is essential for teamwork and professional growth. In your opinion, is the trend toward remote work more beneficial for society, or are we losing something important?
(pause for 45-second response)

Interviewer: Thanks for those insights. Just one last question. Some experts suggest that because technology allows us to work from anywhere at any time, the "boundary" between our professional lives and personal lives is disappearing. Do you think organizations should implement strict rules—like banning work emails after 6:00 PM—to protect employees' personal time? Why or why not?
(pause for 45-second response)

Answer/Explanation:

Potential answers to the questions could be:

Interviewer: Hi there! Thank you for participating in our study. To start, could you tell me about a time you had to complete a project or a difficult task? Where did you choose to work—was it a library, a quiet office, or maybe a busy cafe? Why did you pick that specific location?

Sample Response: "Last semester, I had to write a twenty-page research paper for my history class. I actually chose to work in a very quiet corner of the university library. I picked that spot because my dorm room was way too noisy, and I knew that if I stayed home, I'd probably just end up taking a nap or watching TV. Being surrounded by other people who were also studying really helped me stay on task."

Linguistic Explanation: This response is effective because it uses the past tense correctly ("chose," "was," "had to"). It directly answers all parts of the prompt: the task, the location, and the reason.

Interviewer: That's interesting. People often have strong preferences regarding their surroundings. Some people feel they are most productive when they are entirely alone in a silent room, while others prefer having some background noise or people around them. Which environment do you prefer when you really need to focus, and why does that work for you?

Sample Response: "I definitely prefer a little bit of background noise. If it's too silent, every tiny sound—like a clock ticking—distracts me. I usually go to a small coffee shop near my house. The 'white noise' of the espresso machine and people talking quietly actually helps me enter a 'flow state.' It makes me feel less isolated while I'm working on difficult assignments."

Linguistic Explanation: This response uses comparative logic ("too silent," "less isolated"). It uses specific vocabulary like "white noise" and "flow state," which demonstrates a higher range of vocabulary.

Interviewer: Excellent. Now, let's look at a broader trend. Many companies are now allowing employees to work from home permanently. Proponents argue this increases job satisfaction and saves time. However, others claim that working in a shared physical office is essential for teamwork and professional growth. In your opinion, is the trend toward remote work more beneficial for society, or are we losing something important?

Sample Response: "That's a great question. I think remote work is generally more beneficial. I mean, it reduces traffic congestion and gives people more time with their families since they don't have to commute. However, I do think we are losing that 'spontaneous' collaboration you get in an office. But overall, the flexibility it provides for work-life balance is probably more important for our long-term well-being."

Linguistic Explanation: The speaker acknowledges both sides of the argument using transition words ("However," "But overall"). This shows the ability to handle complex, abstract topics.

Interviewer: Thanks for those insights. Just one last question. Some experts suggest that because technology allows us to work from anywhere at any time, the "boundary" between our professional lives and personal lives is disappearing. Do you think organizations should implement strict rules—like banning work emails after 6:00 PM—to protect employees' personal time? Why or why not?

> Sample Response: "Um, I think a strict ban might be too much, but I definitely agree with the idea behind it. People shouldn't feel pressured to answer their boss at dinner. Instead of a 'ban,' maybe companies should just have a 'culture' where it's okay to wait until morning. If you make it a hard rule, it might hurt people who prefer to work late at night because they have kids during the day. So, flexibility is better than a strict law."
>
> Linguistic Explanation: This response shows critical thinking. It offers an alternative (changing "culture" instead of a "ban") and provides a specific example (parents with children) to support the argument.

Preparation Tip for "Take an Interview"

Manage your 45 seconds: Notice that the responses above are about 75–100 words. This is the "sweet spot" for 45 seconds. If you find yourself finishing in 20 seconds, try to add an extra "Why" or a personal example to round out your answer. If you are still talking when the timer stops, try to get to your main point sooner next time!

General Strategies

1. Use "The 1-Second Rule"

   In tasks like *Listen and Repeat*, your brain needs a tiny moment to "save" the audio before your mouth starts moving. In the *Take and Interview* task, this allows you to collect your thoughts briefly.

   - The Tip: After the speaker finishes, wait for about 1 second before you start speaking.
   - Why: This prevents you from "tripping" over the first word and helps you remember the end of the sentence more clearly.

2. Sound Natural

   You should sound like a natural human speaking.

   - The Tip: If you forget a word, use "filler" words like "I mean," "Well," or "You know."
   - Why: Silence is your enemy. Using a filler word to keep the conversation moving while you think of what to say next.

3. The "Why" Is More Important Than the "What"

   In the *Take an Interview* task, students often spend too much time describing *what* happened and forget to explain *why* it matters.

   - The Tip: Always try to use the word "because" in every answer.
   - Example: Don't just say, "I like the library." Say, "I like the library because it is quiet and helps me focus."

4. Chunking (Grouping Words)

   Don't try to remember 15 individual words. It's too hard!

   - The Tip: Group words into small "packets" of meaning.
   - Example:
     - *Hard way:* "The" + "library" + "is" + "closed" + "on" + "Sundays."
     - *Easy way:* "The library" + "is closed" + "on Sundays."
   - Why: This makes you sound more rhythmic and helps your memory work better.

More Practice

Question 1: Listen and Repeat

Listen to ***Audio File #14*** *in your online companion.*

Scenario Context: A new student is receiving an orientation from a library assistant.

Visual Setting: A large circulation desk with computer monitors, bookshelves in the background, and a sign that reads "Quiet Study Area."

Question 2: Listen and Repeat

Listen to ***Audio File #15*** *in your online companion.*

Scenario Context: A student is speaking with a dining hall coordinator about meal plans and facilities.

Visual Setting: A modern cafeteria with a salad bar, digital menu boards, and a card scanner at the entrance.

Question 3: Take an Interview

Listen to ***Audio File #17*** *in your online companion.*

Question 4: Take an Interview

Listen to ***Audio File #18*** *in your online companion.*

Answers and Explanations

Question 1:

SEQUENCE	FULL SENTENCE	LINGUISTIC FOCUS & COMMON PITFALLS
1	Your student ID card acts as your library card.	"Student ID card" and "library card" should be spoken without long pauses between words.
2	Most textbooks are located on the second floor.	"Are located" requires clear pronunciation of the "-ed" ending.
3	You can borrow up to 10 books at a time.	"Up to" and "at a time" are common idiomatic fillers.
4	If a book is unavailable, you may request it through our interlibrary loan system.	"Interlibrary loan" is a term that requires steady pacing.
5	Please be aware that laptops and tablets must remain on silent mode while you are in the reading room.	The phrase starting with "while" adds a layer of time-based context you must retain.
6	Private study rooms are available for reservation, but they must be booked at least 24 hours in advance.	The "but" creates a shift in the sentence; ensure your intonation reflects this contrast.
7	Although the main stacks stay open until midnight, the specialized archives and rare book collection close promptly at 5:00 PM.	This sentence tests your memory of two distinct facts: the midnight closing and the 5:00 PM closing.

Key Takeaways for This Scenario

- Specificity of Time: In Sentences 6 and 7, numbers like "24 hours" and "5:00 PM" are high-priority details. Accuracy is important.
- The "Although" Pivot: Sentence 7 is a classic "Long Item." To master it, visualize the two different closing times as you hear them. This mental "map" makes it easier to repeat the 18-word sentence without losing your place.
- Intelligibility: Even if you forget a specific word (like "specialized"), keep your speaking rhythm steady.

Question 2:

SEQUENCE	FULL SENTENCE	LINGUISTIC EXPLANATION
1	Welcome to the main campus dining commons.	Treat "Dining Commons" as a name; keep the words grouped together.
2	You must swipe your card before entering the hall.	"Swipe" is a context-specific functional verb. Ensure the "p" sound is clear.
3	Fresh fruit and salads are prepared every morning.	Pay close attention to the "s" in "salads"—missing plural markers is a common error.
4	If you have dietary restrictions, please speak with our head chef.	"Dietary restrictions" is a high-level academic phrase common in campus life tasks.
5	Students are encouraged to use the reusable containers to help reduce campus waste.	"Are encouraged to use" tests your ability to process longer verb chains.
6	Our weekend brunch is served from ten in the morning until two in the afternoon.	This sentence uses "from/until" phrases that test rhythmic consistency.
7	While the main grill closes during the afternoon, the deli and soup stations remain open until dinner.	The word "While" signals a comparison; the challenge is remembering the status of both "the grill" and "the deli."

To improve your performance:

- Keep in mind your two goals: (1) accurate repetition; (2) clearly intelligible. Don't rush to speak for the sake of accurate repetition if it means you will sacrifice clarity. They are both important.
- Don't over-focus on single words: If you get stuck on the word "reusable," don't let it ruin the rest of the sentence. Keep the sentence structure intact, as the scoring looks for overall intelligibility and sentence flow.

Question 3:

Interviewer: Thanks for joining us. To begin, could you describe a recent trip you took using public transportation, like a bus or a train? Where were you going, and what was the experience like for you?

Sample Response: "Last weekend, I actually took the subway to go to a professional baseball game in the city center. I chose the train because parking near the stadium is always a nightmare and it's super expensive. The experience was pretty good—it was a bit crowded with other fans, but everyone was in a great mood. It took about 30 minutes, and I really liked that I could just relax and listen to music instead of dealing with traffic."

Linguistic Explanation: This response accurately uses past-tense markers ("took," "was," "liked") and provides a logical "cause and effect" for the choice (avoiding expensive parking).

Interviewer: That's helpful. When it comes to getting around, some people prefer the privacy and flexibility of driving their own car, while others prefer the convenience of public transit or walking. Which mode of transportation do you prefer for your daily commute, and why?

Sample Response: "I definitely prefer walking whenever it's possible. Even though driving is faster, I find that walking to my classes helps me wake up in the morning and gives me some light exercise. It's also a great way to save money on gas and car insurance. If the weather is really bad, I might take the bus, but honestly, having that quiet time to clear my head while walking is my favorite part of the day."

Linguistic Explanation: This response uses conditional structures ("whenever it's possible," "If the weather is bad") and comparative reasoning ("even though driving is faster").

Interviewer: Interesting. Now, looking at the bigger picture, many cities are considering "pedestrian-only" zones, where cars are completely banned from certain downtown areas to reduce pollution and noise. Do you think this is a good strategy for modern cities, or does it create too many problems for businesses and commuters?

Sample Response: "I think pedestrian-only zones are a fantastic idea for the environment. When you remove cars, the air quality improves and the area becomes much safer for families. However, I can see why local businesses might worry about losing customers who drive from far away. To make it work, the city would need to provide really efficient shuttle buses. So, I agree with the strategy, but only if there is a good plan for those who still need to get downtown."

Linguistic Explanation: This response demonstrates complexity by acknowledging a counter-argument ("I can see why . . .") before reaffirming the original stance.

Interviewer: One last question. Some researchers suggest that in the future, high-speed internet and virtual reality will make physical travel for meetings or vacations unnecessary. Do you agree that digital experiences will eventually replace the need for physical travel? Why or why not?

Sample Response: "I don't think digital experiences can ever fully replace the real thing. I mean, you can see a 3D image of a beach or a famous museum, but you can't feel the ocean breeze or smell the food in a foreign country. Technology is great for a quick business meeting because it saves money, but for personal experiences and vacations, humans have a natural desire to actually 'be' there. So, I think physical travel will always be important."

Linguistic Explanation: This response uses sensory details ("ocean breeze," "smell the food") to support an abstract argument, which is a high-level speaking skill on the TOEFL.

Pacing Advice: If you find you have 5 seconds left, add a "closing signal" like: *"That's basically my view on the matter"* or *"So, that's why I feel that way."*

Question 4:

Interviewer: Hi! Thanks for helping us out. To start, could you tell me about a time you tried to be more environmentally friendly? For example, did you start recycling, or maybe you chose to stop using plastic water bottles? What exactly did you do, and was it difficult to maintain?

Sample Response: "About a year ago, I decided to stop buying plastic water bottles entirely. I bought a high-quality metal flask and started carrying it with me everywhere on campus. At first, it was a little bit difficult to remember to bring it with me in the morning, and sometimes I would leave it in a classroom by accident. But after a few weeks, it just became a habit. I really liked that I was saving money and not creating so much trash every day."

Linguistic Explanation: This response effectively uses sequence markers ("About a year ago," "At first," "But after . . .") to tell a clear, chronological story.

Interviewer: That's great to hear. When it comes to being "green," some people find it easy to change their daily habits, while others find it very inconvenient or expensive. Do you personally find it easy or difficult to make eco-friendly choices in your life? Why is that?

Sample Response: "I'd say it's a mix, but generally, I find it a bit difficult. As a student, I'm always on a tight budget and I'm usually in a rush between classes. Sometimes the 'green' option, like buying organic food or sustainable clothing, is way more expensive than the regular version. Also, it's not always convenient to find a recycling bin when I'm walking across campus. So, while I want to help the planet, my schedule and my budget often get in the way."

Linguistic Explanation: This uses concessive language ("While I want to help . . . my budget gets in the way"), which shows a high level of grammatical control.

Interviewer: Interesting point. Now, many universities are considering a "zero-waste" policy, where all single-use plastics—like soda bottles and plastic utensils—are completely banned from campus dining halls. Do you think this is an effective way to protect the environment, or is it too restrictive for students who are in a hurry?

> Sample Response: "I think a zero-waste policy is a very bold and necessary move. If the university provides alternatives, like wooden forks or compostable containers, then it's not really that restrictive. Sure, it might take a few days for students to get used to the change, but the amount of plastic waste it would prevent is huge. I believe that institutions have a responsibility to lead by example, even if it causes a minor inconvenience for the students at first."

> Linguistic Explanation: The speaker uses strong adjectives ("bold," "necessary," "compostable") to convey a firm stance, which is key for expressing an opinion.

Interviewer: Just one more. Some experts argue that individual actions, like recycling or saving water, don't actually matter compared to the pollution caused by large corporations. They suggest we should focus on government regulations instead of individual habits. Do you agree that individual efforts are less important than large-scale policy changes? Why or why not?

> Sample Response: "That's a complex issue, but I don't think it's an 'either-or' situation. I agree that large-scale government policies have a bigger impact on total pollution levels, but individual efforts are still vital because they change the culture. When millions of people care about recycling, it puts pressure on those big corporations to change their ways. So, while laws are powerful, I think individual actions are the foundation for those laws. We need both to really solve the problem."

> Linguistic Explanation: This response handles a philosophical debate by refusing the "false dilemma" presented in the question, showing "critical thinking" through English.

Final Practice Tip

If you feel yourself getting stuck on an abstract idea, try to use a "filler phrase" like, *"That's a complex issue, but if I had to choose . . ."* to give yourself 3 seconds to think of your main argument!

APPENDIX 1

Self-Evaluation Checklist

Write an Email

☐ I elaborated on my points and expressed them clearly.

☐ I checked whether I used correct social conventions (e.g., politeness, properly worded requests, etc.).

☐ I checked my word choice and use of idioms.

☐ I used a range of syntax and vocabulary.

☐ I checked for grammar errors and spelling errors.

☐ Overall, I addressed the specific task effectively.

Writing for an Academic Discussion

☐ I planned well by summarizing the professor's question to myself and checking the other posts.

☐ I decided on at least two main points to write about that are relevant to the discussion.

☐ I started with a sentence that used opinion language to introduce my point of view.

☐ I used transitions to move from one idea to another.

☐ I was able to conclude without running out of time and had enough time to edit my response.

☐ I expressed my response clearly.

☐ I elaborated on my points with explanations, examples, or details.

☐ I checked my word choice and use of idioms.

☐ I used a range of syntax and vocabulary.

☐ I checked for grammar errors and spelling errors.

Speaking: Listen and Repeat

☐ I tried to repeat the prompt exactly, without missing words.

☐ I paid special attention to the types of function words I sometimes miss.

☐ I did as well with the last part of the prompt as with the first part.

☐ I spoke clearly and paid attention to my pronunciation.

Speaking: Take an Interview

☐ My response was on topic.

☐ My response was well elaborated.

☐ I maintained a good conversational speaking pace.

☐ I made appropriate intentional use of pauses, but I didn't pause much unintentionally.

☐ I spoke clearly and pronounced my words well.

☐ I used rhythm and intonation to help convey meaning.

☐ I used a range of vocabulary and grammar to express myself.

☐ I used transitions to move from one idea to another.

APPENDIX 2

These are the written scripts for the online audio files.

Audio File #1

"I heard the professor is moving the deadline for the research paper up to this Friday—did you catch that too?"

Audio File #2

"I was thinking about joining the intramural soccer league, but I'm worried it might take up too much study time. What do you think?"

Audio File #3

"I'm trying to add the Advanced Statistics course, but the system says I need a 'departmental override.' Do you know where the registrar's office is?"

Audio File #4

Narrator: *Listen to a conversation between two students in the student union.*

Male Student: *Hey Sarah! I didn't see you at the volunteer fair yesterday. I thought you were dying to sign up for the beach clean-up project?*

Female Student: *I was! But by the time I finished my chemistry lab, the fair was packing up. I guess my lab partner and I got a little too carried away with our titration experiment.*

Male Student: That's too bad. The list filled up pretty fast, but I think they're still looking for people to coordinate the carpool for Saturday morning.

Female Student: *Carpool coordinator? Honestly, I have enough trouble keeping my own schedule straight. I was really hoping to just get my hands dirty on the dunes.*

Male Student: *Well, why don't you email Professor Miller? He's overseeing the whole thing. Sometimes people drop out at the last minute because of midterms.*

Female Student: *That's a thought. I'll send him a note tonight—it's worth a shot, right?*

Audio File #5

Narrator: *Listen to a conversation between a student and a campus bookstore employee.*

Student: *Hi, I'm looking for the textbook for Introduction to Environmental Policy. I checked the shelves over there, but I only saw the "Global Politics" section.*

Employee: *Policy . . . let me check the system. Ah, right. That one was moved to the "Special Reserve" shelf behind the counter because the professor recently switched to a newer edition.*

Student: *Oh, no. I actually found a used copy of the previous edition online for half the price. Do you think the changes are significant?*

Employee: *Well, usually it's just a few updated case studies or rearranged chapters. However, for this specific course, the professor mentioned that the new edition includes the updated federal regulations passed last year.*

Student: *That sounds like it might be important for the exams. I guess I'll have to skip the "bargain" version. Do you have any used copies of the new edition yet?*

Employee: *Since the edition just came out, we haven't had any students sell them back yet. But we do have a digital rental option that's much cheaper than the physical hardcover.*

Student: *A digital rental? I've never tried that. I do like highlighting my books, but saving money is my top priority right now.*

Audio File #6

Narrator: *Listen to a conversation between a student and a campus housing coordinator.*

Student: *Hi, I'm sorry to drop in without an appointment, but I just found out my current roommate is graduating early in December.*

Coordinator: *Oh, that's a bit of a surprise mid-semester. Usually, when that happens, the housing office assigns a new student to the vacant spot for the spring term.*

Student: *Right, I figured as much. But I was actually wondering . . . my younger brother was just accepted for the spring semester as a transfer student. Is there any way he could take that spot?*

Coordinator: *It's definitely possible, but it's not as simple as just handing him the key. He needs to have his housing application submitted and his deposit paid by the end of this week.*

Student: *He's already done that! He's just waiting to hear where he'll be placed.*

Coordinator: *In that case, you both need to submit a "Mutual Roommate Request" form through the student portal. Once both forms are in, I can manually link his application to your room number. But you'd better hurry—assignments for transfers start being processed on Monday.*

Student: *Great, I'll call him right now and make sure he logs in tonight. Thanks a million!*

Audio File #7

Narrator: *Listen to an announcement from a university official.*

Official: *"Attention all students currently residing in North Campus dormitories. Due to an unexpected water main break on Main Street, the city will be conducting emergency repairs starting tonight at 11:00 PM. As a result, water service to the Hillside and Riverside residence halls will be temporarily suspended for approximately six hours. We have set up a temporary station in the Student Union lobby where bottled water and hand sanitizer are available free of charge until the repairs are completed. We apologize for the inconvenience and appreciate your patience as the city works to resolve this issue."*

Audio File #8

Narrator: *Listen to an announcement in a university science building.*

Department Head: *"Attention students and faculty. This is a reminder regarding the new safety protocols for the Chemistry and Biology wings. Effective immediately, no food or drink—including bottled water—is* *permitted in any laboratory space. However, due to the upcoming finals week, we have converted the third-floor faculty lounge into a 24-hour study area where refreshments are allowed. Please ensure all lab coats and safety goggles are stored in your assigned lockers before entering the lounge. We appreciate your cooperation in keeping our research environment safe and sterile."*

Audio File #9

Narrator: *Listen to an announcement being made over a university's public address system.*

Official: *"Attention students and staff. Please be advised that starting this Wednesday, the University Shuttle's Blue Line will be suspended due to emergency roadwork on West Campus. During this time, the Gold Line will be rerouted to include stops at the Student Health Center and the Engineering Building. While we expect the Gold Line to remain on its usual 15-minute rotation, we recommend allowing extra travel time during peak morning hours. Regular service on the Blue Line is expected to resume by Friday afternoon. For real-time updates on bus locations, please consult the 'Campus Transit' mobile app. Thank you for your cooperation."*

Audio File #10

Narrator: *Listen to a talk in a business and economics class.*

Professor: *"When we look at why some companies thrive while others fail, we often turn to the 'Resource-Based View' of the firm. This theory suggests that a company's success isn't just about the industry it's in, but rather the unique resources it controls.*

To be a source of sustained competitive advantage, a resource must meet four specific criteria, often called the VRIO framework. First, the resource must be ***Valuable****—it has to help the firm exploit an opportunity or neutralize a threat. Second, it must be* ***Rare****; if everyone has it, it's just a requirement for entry, not a competitive edge. Third, it must be* ***Inimitable****, meaning it's difficult or expensive for competitors to copy. And finally, the firm must be* ***Organized*** *to capture the value of that resource.*

Think of a company with a secret, world-class software algorithm. If that algorithm is valuable and rare, the company has a head start. But if a competitor can easily write a similar code by next week, that advantage is only temporary. It's the 'Inimitable' quality—the difficulty of duplication—that often separates a one-hit wonder from a market leader."

Audio File #11

Narrator: *Listen to a talk in a history class.*

Professor: *"Today we're going to talk about the history of the* ***Silk Road****. Now, despite the name, the Silk Road wasn't just one single road. It was actually a huge network of many different paths that connected China to Europe and the Middle East.*

Why was it so important? Well, for a long time, China was the only place in the world that knew how to make silk. Because silk was soft and beautiful, people in far-away places like Rome wanted to buy it, even though it was very expensive.

But the Silk Road wasn't just about selling cloth. It was a 'cultural bridge.' As traders traveled across mountains and deserts, they didn't just carry goods like silk, spices, and tea. They also shared ***ideas****. For example, this is how the religion of Buddhism spread from India into China. They also shared inventions, like paper-making and gunpowder. So, even though the Silk Road was built for business, its greatest impact was probably the way it helped different cultures learn from each other."*

Audio File #12

Narrator: *Listen to a talk in an environmental science class.*

Professor: *"Today, let's discuss a phenomenon known as the* ***Urban Heat Island effect****. Have you ever noticed that it feels significantly warmer in the center of a city than in the nearby countryside? This isn't just your imagination.*

Cities are often much hotter because of the materials we use to build them. In rural areas, plants and trees provide shade and release moisture into the air, which helps keep things cool. However, in a city, we replace that greenery with dark surfaces like asphalt roads and brick buildings. These materials are excellent at absorbing and trapping heat from the sun during the day. Then, at night, they slowly release that heat back into the air, preventing the city from cooling down.

This extra heat doesn't just make people uncomfortable; it also increases the demand for air conditioning, which uses more electricity. To combat this, some cities are now creating 'green roofs'—covering the tops of buildings with living plants. These plants act like a natural cooling system, helping to lower the temperature of the entire building and the surrounding air."

Audio File #13

Narrator: *You are visiting the Career Services Center on campus. Listen to the counselor and repeat what he says. You will have a set amount of time after each sentence to repeat it exactly.*

Man: *We offer several resources for career planning.*

Man: *You can schedule a meeting with an advisor online.*

Man: *If you have a draft of your resume, I can look at it now.*

Man: *Most students find that a mock interview helps reduce their anxiety before the real thing.*

Man: *Our database contains hundreds of local internship opportunities specifically curated for undergraduate students.*

Man: *Please remember that you must register at least 48 hours in advance for the upcoming job fair.*

Man: *Although most workshops are held in this building, the networking seminar on Friday has been moved to the student union.*

Audio File #14

Narrator: *You are at the main university library. Listen to the library assistant and repeat what he says. You will have a set amount of time after each sentence to repeat it exactly.*

Man: *Your student ID card acts as your library card.*

Man: *Most textbooks are located on the second floor.*

Man: *You can borrow up to 10 books at a time.*

Man: *If a book is unavailable, you may request it through our interlibrary loan system.*

Man: *Please be aware that laptops and tablets must remain on silent mode while you are in the reading room.*

Man: *Private study rooms are available for reservation, but they must be booked at least 24 hours in advance.*

Man: *Although the main stacks stay open until midnight, the specialized archives and rare book collection close promptly at five o'clock.*

Audio File #15

Narrator: *You are at the campus dining hall. Listen to the coordinator and repeat what she says. You will have a set amount of time after each sentence to repeat it exactly.*

Woman: *Welcome to the main campus dining commons.*

Woman: *You must swipe your card before entering the hall.*

Woman: *Fresh fruit and salads are prepared every morning.*

Woman: *If you have dietary restrictions, please speak with our head chef.*

Woman: *Students are encouraged to use the reusable containers to help reduce campus waste.*

Woman: *Our weekend brunch is served from ten in the morning until two in the afternoon.*

Woman: *While the main grill closes during the afternoon, the deli and soup stations remain open until dinner.*

Audio File #16

Narrator: *You are participating in a research study about how modern work environments affect productivity and work-life balance. You have agreed to a short online interview. The researcher will now ask you four questions.*

Interviewer: *Hi there! Thank you for participating in our study. To start, could you tell me about a time you had to complete a project or a difficult task? Where did you choose to work—was it a library, a quiet office, or maybe a busy cafe? Why did you pick that specific location?*

Interviewer: *That's interesting. People often have strong preferences regarding their surroundings. Some people feel they are most productive when they are entirely alone in a silent room, while others prefer having some background noise or people around them. Which environment do you prefer when you really need to focus, and why does that work for you?*

Interviewer: *Excellent. Now, let's look at a broader trend. Many companies are now allowing employees to work from home permanently. Proponents argue this increases job satisfaction and saves time. However, others claim that working in a shared physical office is essential for teamwork and professional growth. In your opinion, is the trend toward remote work more beneficial for society, or are we losing something important?*

Interviewer: *Thanks for those insights. Just one last question. Some experts suggest that because technology allows us to work from anywhere at any time, the "boundary" between our professional lives and personal lives is disappearing. Do you think organizations should implement strict rules—like banning work emails after 6:00 PM—to protect employees' personal time? Why or why not?*

Audio File #17

Narrator: *You are a participant in a university research study regarding urban development and how people move around their cities. You have agreed to a short interview. The researcher will now ask you four questions.*

Interviewer: *Thanks for joining us. To begin, could you describe a recent trip you took using public transportation, like a bus or a train? Where were you going, and what was the experience like for you?*

Interviewer: *That's helpful. When it comes to getting around, some people prefer the privacy and flexibility of driving their own car, while others prefer the convenience of public transit or walking. Which mode of transportation do you prefer for your daily commute, and why?*

Interviewer: *Interesting. Now, looking at the bigger picture, many cities are considering "pedestrian-only" zones, where cars are completely banned from certain downtown areas to reduce pollution and noise. Do you think this is a good strategy for modern cities, or does it create too many problems for businesses and commuters?*

Interviewer: *One last question. Some researchers suggest that in the future, high-speed internet and virtual reality will make physical travel for meetings or vacations unnecessary. Do you agree that digital experiences will eventually replace the need for physical travel? Why or why not?*

Audio File #18

Narrator: *You have volunteered to participate in a research study conducted by the University's Environmental Science Department regarding student habits and green policies. The researcher will now ask you four questions.*

Interviewer: *Hi! Thanks for helping us out. To start, could you tell me about a time you tried to be more environmentally friendly? For example, did you start recycling, or maybe you chose to stop using plastic water bottles? What exactly did you do, and was it difficult to maintain?*

Interviewer: *That's great to hear. When it comes to being "green," some people find it easy to change their daily habits, while others find it very inconvenient or expensive. Do you personally find it easy or difficult to make eco-friendly choices in your life? Why is that?*

Interviewer: *Interesting point. Now, many universities are considering a "zero-waste" policy, where all single-use plastics—like soda bottles and plastic utensils—are completely banned from campus dining halls. Do you think this is an effective way to protect the environment, or is it too restrictive for students who are in a hurry?*

Interviewer: *Just one more. Some experts argue that individual actions, like recycling or saving water, don't actually matter compared to the pollution caused by large corporations. They suggest we should focus on government regulations instead of individual habits. Do you agree that individual efforts are less important than large-scale policy changes? Why or why not?*